W9-BZV-357

A   SHEARWATER   BOOK

Night After Night

Night After Night

Diana Starr Cooper

Illustrations by Ivy Starr

ISLAND PRESS / Shearwater Books

Washington, D.C. / Covelo, California

A Shearwater Book
published by Island Press

Copyright © 1994 by Island Press

All rights reserved under International and Pan-American Copyright
Conventions. No part of this book may be reproduced in any form
or by any means without permission in writing from the publisher:
Island Press, Suite 300, 1718 Connecticut Avenue NW,
Washington, D.C. 20009.

Island Press is a trademark of the Center for Resource Economics.

LIBRARY OF CONGRESS CATALOGING-IN-PUBLICATION DATA
Cooper, Diana Starr.
Night after night / Diana Starr Cooper.
p.   cm.
ISBN 1-55963-306-9 (cloth). — ISBN 1-55963-307-7 (pbk.)
1. Circus.   2. Big Apple Circus.   I. Title.
GV1815.C83   1994
791.3—dc20   93-44947
CIP

Printed on recycled, acid-free paper.

Manufactured in the United States of America

10 9 8 7 6 5 4 3 2 1

To Donald J. Olsen,
who knows how to praise

And every minute has an azure tent with silver bells
And every Hour has a bright golden Gate carved with skill
And every Day and Night has walls of brass and Gates of
   adamant
Shining like precious stones and ornamental with
   appropriate signs. . . .
Every time less than a pulsation of the artery
Is Equal in its period and value to Six Thousand Years.

William Blake, *Milton*, 1804

SE NO GHE FUSSE

A dog is walking on the rocks.
If that dog weren't there
coming between me and the rocks
I wouldn't understand this world
I wouldn't.

Fish are swimming in the water
the water flows around the fish
birds are flying in the air
the air moves between them
if there were no fish
if there were no birds
between the water and me
between the air and me
I couldn't live here
I couldn't.

If there were no creatures
in the midst of this desert
I wouldn't stay here
I wouldn't.

Ernesto Calzavara,
Analfabeto, 1979
Translated by T. S. Bergin

Begin with the name — circus, *le cirque*, the ring — forty-two feet, or about thirteen meters, in diameter — the size you need, as Philip Astley discovered in London in 1768, to make the back of a galloping horse most hospitable to a person dancing. The circle entwines laws of centrifugal and centripetal force with the forces and rhythms of the horse, allowing the seemingly impossible actually to occur. The circus as we know it has its origins, and its name's ancestry, in this classical shape of the horse and his rider-dancer, in motion and relation. It is akin to the classic and exact concept of turnout, which gives to the ballet dancer who obeys it the foundation on which to balance and from which to fly. The circus ring, in much the same way, must be correct. It must be exact in size, carefully banked, its footing painstakingly arranged and raked, and all, originally and ultimately, for the horse. Its clay, sand, and sawdust may be periodically covered with cloth or boards; nets and trapezes may be hung above it, for the benefit of human performers; but underneath everything the clay, sand, and sawdust must be there, the ring must be there, for the sake of the horses. And the horses must be there. Otherwise, no circus.

One summer evening I spent several hours, along with about fifteen hundred other people, forming another ring, around the ring of The Big Apple Circus, in performance on the road in Hanover, New Hampshire. From the audience's point of view, the inside of the Big Apple's big blue tent is another circle, and it's important to know that it is both very large and very small: large, in that its height has a skylike quality, azure and star-spangled, and its perimeter becomes a horizon, the limit of the known world; small, in that you're not alone in there, by any means. You're part of a crowd, at close quarters. The faces, the applause, shrieks, stomping, murmurings, whistling, especially the rapt, breathless silences, of everyone around you, become yours, because you are all in tiers of closely concentric circles. It's a good thing to have everyone turned toward the geometric center, because each person helps the circle hold, and everyone is also thus encircled.

It's important to remember—impossible to forget, when you're there—that this world is ephemeral. Circuses were traditionally itinerant; they happened in tents; they had to be able to move from place to place. Modern technology makes the Big Apple tent fireproof and allows for the construction, dismantlement, and transport of what is really an immense structure: five stories high, it is, and 137 feet in diameter. Seen from across a field at night, with its swags of white lights scalloped from mast to mast against the sky, it looks like an ocean liner far out on the water. Yet it is still a tent. It appears on Monday in what, on Sunday, was an empty field. While it's there, it forms the landscape around it in a new way, transforming its meanings just as horses do when they walk into a pasture. A week later, there's an empty field again. The tent is gone, and so is the little village of trucks and trailers that clustered around it as if it were a castle. Did I dream it? This can't happen, of course, when a show leaves Madison Square Garden. I suppose you might experience something similar if you were to linger after the opera was over, gazing in silence at the empty stage where what was vividly there is there no longer. But circus carries this mysterious phenomenon, of art as a dis-

appearing act, to an extreme. The annual appearance of the Big Apple Circus tent, with its neighboring trucks, trailers, horse and elephant stalls, in Damrosch Park, right next to the Metropolitan Opera House in Lincoln Center — and their subsequent annual disappearance — epitomize this phenomenon in an especially vivid way. Afterward the Met stays on, a bare white cliff looming over an empty little clearing at its foot.

No one in the Big Apple Circus audience is very far from what goes on in the ring, and once again a classic set of constraints assists in, may in fact be central to, the art. The tent holds seventeen hundred people, and the farthest seat in the bleachers is only fifty feet from the ring. The result is not merely a feeling of being close to everything that happens, but an actual physical fact, the space calculated to place just the right number of demands, but no more than we can accommodate, on our senses. On the other hand, it is impossible to watch a three-ring circus. You're in the middle of a gigantic machine with a thousand moving parts. You can catch glimpses, snatches, of what goes on, but you're in a state of incessant distraction. No focus is allowed. The one-ring circus invites focus, and you get to do it yourself, without intervention.

I've often wondered whether people schooled in what's known as nature photography, with its insistence on the closeup shot of, say, a bird (every bright immobile feather an inch away, its glinting eye fixed forever in time) are disheartened, rather than inspired, by the golden flash that's an oriole flying from one tree to another fifty yards away.

Using their own power, and subject to real time and space, people in the circus audience sit near the edges of their seats. They lean forward. The arrangement of spaces in the tent awakens all the senses, summoning you to attend to each and every moment and to go with them all as they parade by one after another. Then you can return the gaze of the camel's eye and hear, above or below the music, the horses' snorting and the insistent hollow drumming of their hoofbeats. Elephants smell, deliciously, of elephants. Beautiful ladies sweat.

What happens is very curious. I know of no other aesthetic experience wherein you are so little apt to wonder what time it is, how your children are, whether your foot itches, how your marriage is going, whether we will see peace in our time. People attending the great Greek dramas in their amphitheaters may have experienced something of this transformation from isolated spectators to intimately united and fully conscious witnesses. At the circus, which involves all the senses, you are carried away, and you are all there.

Tonight, in rural New Hampshire, you're part of a pretty monochromatic crowd, but down on the Big Apple's home turf, in the boroughs of New York City, you'll be part of a gathering that looks and sounds like an eccentric, merry United Nations. Wherever you go, there will be lots of children. In America we seem to think that having a child or two at our side is a prerequisite of admission to the circus. In Europe (and increasingly at Lincoln Center, I'm happy to see) people understand that aesthetic joy is not the sole property of the young. In supposedly staid Geneva, I've seen the Circus Knie tent fill to capacity, every evening, with adults dressed as for the opera, and not a child in sight.

The audience in Hanover tonight is exuberant and expressive. The audience's responsiveness, and the fact that there's no secret about it, is of immense importance to the performers. Soon we shall see what the performers look like, to us. But first imagine, for a moment, what it's like for a performer to go into the bright little ring, with its surrounding landscape — right there! — of faces, hands, bodies; to enter a circumference of palpable energy.

The space they come from, backstage, is no more than twenty by thirty feet. It's dark. There's a lot going on back there. Every square foot and every second are allotted. An extra person allowed in to observe the scene has to be carefully instructed where to stand, and told that she may by no means stray from that spot. Were she to move randomly or impulsively, she might step into the two-foot square where an acrobat does handstand pushups before going on, or move too close to the rope, one of a welter, that operates the second curtain, or block access to a pair of boots standing ready for someone to leap into them, fireman style. No one must get in the way of the horses, who stand lined up, side by side, shifting their feet and tossing their heads, awaiting their cue.

When the elephants are brought in there, one night, I can't see them at first; it's too dark. I realize only that the whole space has filled with a fragrant shape, a looming solidified shadow, Anna May. Darlene Williams is mounted on Anna May, up near the ceiling, and behind them, Darlene's daughter, Stormy, four years old, sits six feet up on little Ned, a baby elephant. Beside them stands Ben Williams, husband and father of the riders; he handles the elephants. Silence, or close to it; only distant laughter as the clown act proceeds in the ring on the other side of the curtain. The dim air feels heavy, alive. The child leans intently forward, ready. Suddenly, Rimsky-Korsakov's trumpet fanfare rings out, the curtains sweep aside, and the elephants plunge forward into a flare of silver light as if they were parting the waters. The little elephant and the little girl lurch and dive forward into that light. With the stirring music comes the oceanic welcome of the crowd.

When the people out there are happy, there's a massive, positive atmosphere of adrenaline high, back here. A performer said to me once, "Sure, it's powerful. Sometimes it's so strong it's hard to know where you are in it." When, on odd occasions, the audience seems morose, slow to arousal, the people in the ring know it as a sort of bad weather which they will turn themselves inside out to change, like shamans. The exchange of emotion, between performers and audience, back and forth, is so intimate and constant that it feels like an absolute and physical fact in the life of the ring.

However it goes — each night is a new one — there will

be no secrets. There will be mysteries, but no lies. This is because the ring is for horses, and the exact geometries of a horse's way of going are incapable of lying. In the ring designed for horses, the truths of what was once called Natural Philosophy—of motion, gravity, the senses—govern in absolute orders.

Paul Binder, cofounder and artistic director of The Big Apple Circus, and also its ringmaster, once told me something which I believe has to do with how circus works. "Circus," he said, "is the art form most closely involved with the relationship between animals and people." I agree, and I think too that circus is the art form most directly concerned with exploring the conundrum and fact of people *as* animals. Surely all of this is the source of the intense consciousness in the ring and around it. This particular show—the overture from the band is blaring in crescendo, the houselights are dimming—owes its perfection to the extraordinary extent of its exploration of these ideas of people with animals, and of people as animals.

The ringmaster skips into the ring and strides in the spotlight. This is a big man. It's a long, impressive way from

the top of his black top hat—which he sweeps off with a grand gesture—to the toe of his shiny black boot, pointed in a courtly bow—the same kind of boots, with brown tops, that men still wear foxhunting. In between—below the curly hair and the face with oversized and mobile features—we see a white stock tie, a vest covered by a broad-shouldered red tailcoat, and a long-legged pair of creamy riding breeches. This entire getup, the familiar ringmaster iconography, is actually a replica of formal nineteenth-century riding dress. The scarlet coat is properly called Pink, in honor of the London tailor who is said to have designed it. The top hat, Pink coat, and top boots can still be seen at a formal meet of a foxhunt, and those who have represented their country as members of the U.S. equestrian team at the world championships or Olympic games are still entitled to wear a scarlet riding jacket whenever they compete. Most people today, seeing this flamboyant-looking fellow, would say, "He looks like a ringmaster." But a hundred or a hundred and fifty years ago, he'd have been immediately recognized as a superior horseman.

Paul Binder has seldom sat on a horse in his life, but he's dressed the way he is because he's the king of this movable realm in which the horse is traditionally the power and the glory and the center of everything.

It's necessary, inevitable, that he be there. The ring requires a host. We need to hear someone say, in tones of genial formality, "Welcome to The Big Apple Circus!" and, in effect, welcome to my house, welcome to my stable, meet my friends. His voice is deep, full of authority, but full of boyish enthusiasm too. There's a hint of Brooklyn somewhere in his accent that makes him seem like someone we met and got to know long ago. Welcome, he seems to say, to a real but invented world.

The ring needs a teacher, too, a guide to proper behavior. He reminds the audience not to take flash pictures, which could endanger the performers by dazzling them. Later, he'll ask the audience for moments of silence, not just for dramatic effect, but to protect the performers at dangerous points of concentration.

Most important of all, the ring requires a Greek chorus, someone to make its extremes tolerable. Without the ringmaster in command, the unmediated reality of circus would be unbearable. In the theater, there's someone pretending to be someone. In the circus, a real man is on that highwire, nineteen feet above the ground without a net. He's really himself, he's really up there, and he can fall, because gravity is a fact. The artists are surrounded by an audience praying for them but also egging them on, and for us, sitting so near them, it's crucial that the ringmaster step forward, ask for silence, and stand as spotter — poised, still, face upturned and serious — looking out, really, for us all.

For all his vaunted importance, the ringmaster portrays himself as subservient to the performers, although he conducts their measures. His courtly manner, when he introduces them or calls them back for a bow, lets us know that he believes they're the best in the world at what they do. His own grandeur takes second place to his evident pride in those with whom he keeps company.

Importantly, this is also a master who allows himself to be laughed at, although the provocations and interruptions he suffers at the hands of the clowns aren't events he allows so much as accepts as inevitable, the way a kindly person submits, with a sigh, to the importunities of a familiar child.

In short, the ringmaster may look like a splendid anachronism, but this master's role is complicated. It has to do with what makes the circus work, and this is true offstage as well as in the ring.

At six-thirty one October morning, while a gray dawn shower stirs the leaves left on the trees in Damrosch Park,

I'm sitting on a ledge alongside a deserted pathway, waiting for people who don't know I'm here to wake up. On the road, on the roomy summer lots, the trailers cluster and straggle in somewhat random ways, shaping rambling lanes and byways. Here, where space is tight, the perfectly aligned trailer walls form straight and narrow village streets. This village is not medieval; as my friend Bianca observed, it's Renaissance: it looks as though it was built, like Pienza, by the pope. A groom neatly hangs her pitchfork after feeding the horses their breakfasts and mucking out the last stall. Now her broom goes swish, swish. A couple of birds chirp; the leaves rustle in the rain. A security guard saunters by and stops to chat. I tell him I'm waiting for Paul, and he says he hasn't seen him yet. "It's unusual," he says, shaking his head. "He's always up wandering around this place at four every morning. Like clockwork. You know, *checking up on things*."

The circus is an ordered space wherein everyone must adhere to a multitude of laws, all the way from the law of gravity to those regarding the maintenance of civic peace and safety. The master in charge of all this frees that title from the demons of slavery and paternalistic dominance which have come to haunt it, and restores the notion of mastery which has to do with real achievement, and with the responsibility, burden, and glory of teaching, leading, and inspiring. In fact, this is a community which shares the conviction that each person must strive to be good at what he or she does — better than you or I — and not by accident or luck. Such people possess real and legitimate power on which their very lives may depend. Simply because there's so much at stake, and because everyone depends on everyone else, mastery here is not a threat, but a necessity and a pleasure, founded on trust and relying on the order of things.

This is why I always do a double take whenever I hear someone describe a situation of out-of-control craziness as "a circus." One must look elsewhere for an accurate metaphor for chaos. The circus is the most civilized place I know.

The ringmaster represents the necessity, grandeur, and weight of certain hierarchies, which exist for the sake of our well-being and the survival of those whom he introduces, who are, people and other animals both, in their own eccentric ways, masters as well. He is here to lead us into a kind of understanding that all of us here, in all our diversity — not just of race or background or age or sex, but of species as well — all of us are in this together. He's the one person in the ring who knows how it all connects, who makes it all come together and make sense. Everything about his presence represents his sense of duty to a higher intention, and we need him.

The world being the way it is, however, he won't be able to operate in lordly solitude for long. A flapping figure in a burnoose has just scampered in and is hopping from one foot to another and frantically waving his arms about.

On the face of it, Mr. Stubs is a sad sort of clown, but he's more complicated than that. His wide, hooded eyes take everything in. Wistful, wondering, yearning, always in the way or a little bit in the wrong place at the wrong time, Mr. Stubs is always slightly to one side of, and uncomprehending of, what's going on, though insistent upon, and often profoundly right about, his own skewed view of the world. He's the Platonic child. His clothes and floppy hat look like hand-me-downs, loose and shabby. He's also enough like a bum to arouse associations with the other people among us, besides children, who live near the bottom of the social totem pole but who have an acute perception of the world as seen from down there.

Mr. Stubs's character is complex, by turns innocent, knowing, naive, crafty, contemplative, jubilant. He is the ring's Huckleberry Finn — gullible and wise, fooling and fooled, all in the same tattered, chimerical form.

He scurries up to the ringmaster, listens for a moment — bobbing with impatience like an antsy kid who just can't wait — and then, unable to stand it for even one more second, he cries, "Mr. Paul! Mr. Paul!" ("Mister" is the circus honorific. You may be on a first-name basis here, but certain forms are observed nonetheless.) Once upon a time, before they invented Mr. Paul and Mr. Stubs, Paul Binder and Michael Christensen were juggling partners, and the spirit from that other kind of exchange shines forth in their conversation: the one, tall, elegant, speaking in a measured rumble; the other, stooped and raggedy, his voice piping and agitated.

"Mr. Paul! Mr. Paul! Hi, sir! You're not going to believe —"

"Hi, Mr. Stubs." He turns to the audience. "You all know Mr. Stubs, don't you?" He has lovely manners.

"Oh, hi," Mr. Stubs blurts to the audience, like a kid forced to shake hands; then he pokes his face back at Mr. Paul. "Sir, sir, you're not going to *believe* —"

"Mr. Stubs," sternly, but kindly, "how many times

have I told you not to interrupt me when I'm addressing the audience?"

"Oh, gee, sir, you must have told me at least a thousand times."

"A thousand times," Mr. Paul agrees, nodding regretfully.

"Sorry, sir." Mr. Stubs looks around, hunches his shoulders self-consciously.

"Ladies and gentlemen!" Mr. Paul resumes, "we have prepared a very special show for you tonight —"

Mr. Stubs just can't stand it. "You're not going to believe what's going on back there! People are wrapping towels around their heads — and — they've got little pointy shoes on — and they want me to wear this night-gown —"

The ringmaster becomes even taller, puts his hands on his hips. "How many interruptions does *this* make?"

Mr. Stubs considers. "A thousand and one . . ."

"That's it!" Mr. Paul is pleased to find a way to explain everything. "A thousand and one!"

"A thousand and one *what*?" Mr. Stubs doesn't get it.

"A Thousand and One Nights at The Big Apple Circus!"

The show's theme comes from the story of Scheherazade, which is lovely, but also terrifying, if you stop to think about it. The Grand Vizier, as you may recall—who this time takes the shape of a particularly cold, languid, slick sort of Grade B sheik in dark glasses—had been making a career of killing off scores of women, one a night. Scheherazade's inspiration for breaking this grisly pattern was to tell him a different story every night, without giving him the ending of it. The next evening she'd tell him how last night's story came out, and then quickly she'd begin another—again and again luring him to forget all his other plans. The stories which Scheherazade told were strange, mysterious, ominous, involving genies, caves, exotic locales, weird characters, some human but not human. The events were uniformly scary, with consistently satisfactory outcomes. And the Grand Vizier was arrested in what must have become a boring, bloody repetition by a greater desire: to know what came next. In other words, she got him really to pay attention. The brilliance of the circus may have a lot to do with its origins in making people forget whatever else they had in mind and to become fully conscious in the moment.

In the circus, Scheherazade glides around the circle with an ornate book in her arms, luring the sheik, and the audience, into one story after another, that is, one act after another. In the process, we pay attention in just about every way we have of paying attention, including delight, of course, but also fear; laughter, but also anxiety; anticipation, but also moments close to revulsion; tension, relief. In this sense, attention is a working definition of excitement. We attend, throughout, with our whole bodies.

The traditional circus begins with a charivari, an elaborate, noisy celebration which wakes us right up, gets us going. This one, beginning in eerie moonlight to the sound of one mysterious flute, and then bursting forth into bright desert sunlight and a riot of music, involves the whole company. Clad in brilliant costumes, turbans, masks, and veils, a seeming multitude whirls and dashes about, dancing and tumbling in a bizarre, bazaarlike gathering which includes even a manic, dancing tent. Then this cacophonous procession disappears, in a running, leaping chain like the game of crack-the-whip, and the camel caravan appears.

Have you seen a camel lately — I mean really seen one? I should say, have you been with a camel lately, if ever? The *Oxford English Dictionary* tells us that it is "a large hornless ruminant quadruped having humped back, long

neck, and large cushioned feet. The music accompanying
the Big Apple's camels galumphs as if reinforcing this definition. There are six of them, and in a small space that is
a great many camels. They have mobile, velvety lips, perfectly formed for a sneer, and great brown eyes with an
expression both melting and aloof. They seem to scan lim-

itless space, their necks craning above our heads. Their way of moving, a sort of disjointed shamble, makes you think they may actually be composed of several people disguised as a camel, as in the ancient hobbyhorse pantomime. But at the same time you know they really are themselves, because they are thumping and grunting and lalloping along; and also they smell like camels — that is, you learn what that is like. You become, in fact, intensely involved in learning all about camels, in a very short time.

They are infinitely appealing because they are so clearly animals, golden brown and tufty, and comical in the extreme, but also because even though you may not know much about camels you can tell right away that a Liberty act with camels is an unusual, if not impossible, phenomenon. Liberty acts traditionally belong to horses, moving "at liberty," that is, not under saddle, but at the seemingly magical bidding of the trainer in the center of the ring. Liberty and camels are two things you don't usually expect — or want — in the same place at the same time.

Around and around they trot (if you can call it that), in single file, in pairs, then all abreast; they change directions in lurching pirouettes; they lie down, then stand up, on command. They wear enchanting red saddle blankets and tasseled halters. But despite all this culture, they give off an unmistakable air of only just barely doing what they do — an air of willful disorder only temporarily, and not quite, arranged. It's always, with them, a near thing.

For all their furry appeal, the camels' movements and attitudes, at this range, are verging so closely on the chaotic that you don't think, How cute; you think, To know them is — to know them. They don't look dangerous (although I don't doubt that it's a good idea to watch your step and know exactly what you're doing, in their neighborhood). They look goofy; and they look cynical, which is even more interesting. We are not used to this.

I wonder, when did animals become the property of children? How did they come to be considered small, cuddly, stuffed toys, fit company for the nursery? There's Teddy Roosevelt's bear, of course, and Pooh, Bambi, and Babar. Teddy and Pooh are not bears, any more than Babar, eating croissants in his well-tailored green suit, his children wheeled about in perambulators, is an elephant. (Babar's face is as human as his tailoring; we engage him frontally, his trunk being little more than a big nose. But the brows and trunks of real elephants are very unsettling to humans seeking the usual — for us —*face-en-face* encounter with another creature.) And of course Mickey Mouse is no mouse at all, but an art deco imp in white gloves, a vaudevillian with big ears who drives fast cars and talks funny.

The further we've moved, in this century, away from daily proximity to, and relationship with, real animals, the more we have altered, sanitized, desexualized, and humanized their images, to make them safe company for the young, with whom we seem to think they belong. In a perverse sort of reversal, many people now seem to want to alter real animals to fit this altered imagery. When, for example, dogs exhibit ordinary canine behavior instead of the endearing (also unreal, not alive) traits of stuffed toys, many people react with dislike, even viciously. The pressure is on The First Friend to become an object with a body lacking genitals and a head full of fluff. Who would want such a friend?

For thousands of years before our century, animals were the daily working companions of grown men and women, and worthy of respect; or they were mysterious creatures commanding veneration, awe, sometimes fear. The imagery of animals was shaped by those who trained animals to work with them side by side and by priests, shamans, artists, and poets — all learned adults, not superstitious fools or children. The shape-shifters in Native American ceremonies, those who become, magically, coyote, eagle, bear, are not safe companions for children. Neither, for that matter, were centaurs, satyrs, or fauns. Pegasus and Bucephalus were not cute ponies.

The animals in the Thousand and One Nights of The Big Apple Circus are by no stretch of the imagination stuffed animals or toys. Those camels are *camels*. The show puts them close to us, in motion, so that they can show their full size and glory. It takes these camels out of the nursery into the ring right before us, where they are absolutely real. With ordinary imagery swept away, we can be fascinated by them as they are and on our own.

At one point, a camel emerged from the chorus line to do a hilarious combination of break-dance and airs-above-the-ground, bucking and leaping almost in time to the music. His attendant, a harem-costumed girl, responded by doing a belly dance in front of him while she reached for, and repeatedly failed to grab, his halter. Eventually, he subsided. Later I asked his trainer whether that incident had been planned, and he said it had not.

I'm not sure that I believe him, but I'm also not sure that it matters. In one sense, my two-minute acquaintance with the camels made me believe that this breakaway was just the sort of thing one might expect of them. If this was a true instance of naughtiness, then I learned something about camel self-expression when it goes out of bounds. On the other hand, perhaps this was not a spontaneous event, but a variation on the old performance theme of The Naughty Animal. Jokes in animal acts are sometimes about animals refusing to obey us, mocking our self-importance, and it is notoriously difficult, an artistic challenge, to train an animal to enact a convincing charade of disobedience. If this was the case with the camel, not only was the joke excellently told; it also told me something wonderful about the intelligence and skill, self-expression of another kind, of the particular camel who performed it.

Circus work is art; it's not going to show its whole hand to members of the audience. But regardless of my indecision on this matter — or perhaps because of it — I find myself being more intensely interested in and aware of camels than I've ever been before.

Just as you've got used to — not tired of, just very alive

to — these living breathing oddities, a human being appears — a scantily clad and perfectly formed woman, doing a sensuously convincing belly dance around the ring. A great many people of different sizes and shapes turn up in the course of this show, in various stages of brilliant dress and brilliant undress. This beautiful woman is black. As the show proceeds, you become aware that people come in a variety of colors. There are performers from China, a troupe of Moroccan tumblers, three dancing gauchos from Argentina. In the ring, everyone is exposed, heightened, illuminated, and you realize anew that our kind comes in a myriad of shades. The closeness of the view and the seminakedness of the performers reveal this diversity with particular brilliance. But something else is surely also at work to make this awareness occur, something that began with the whirlwind bazaar, that continued, *forte*, with the camels, and that absolutely shines every time animals appear in the show. They perform the aesthetic equivalent of clearing the palate. Their curious shapes, movements, the texture of their fur and skin, awaken us to all shape and movement and richness. They say, The world is rich, various, odd. Wake up, attend to details; anything can happen.

It does. The glamorous belly dancer reaches up, catches a pair of rings, is swept up into the air high above the arena. The lights go out, except for a single silver spot fixed on her. This is the first of several times you will see someone in the air, flying, and you are transfixed, every time. You crane your head back, your mouth drops open a little. She swings, one spot of flying light in the dark expanse near the roof. Then the music soars, she plummets earthward, the full lights pour on to show that she has landed, sitting beautifully, *on an elephant*. WHERE DID THAT ELEPHANT COME FROM? Well, you know all about magic shows, about how there's really a rational explanation for every trick, because you know very well that the elephant came out in the dark and you just didn't notice, you weren't paying attention because you were busy watching the girl in the silver spotlight and that's how they did it. Nonetheless, you and everyone else turn to the next person, shaking your heads and grinning, and you say over and over, "*Where did that elephant come from?*"

Not the least of the joy comes from the reassurance that when a woman plummets earthward, she will be borne up again. Who better, to catch you when you fall, than someone completely dependable, amply large (much larger, even, than she needs to be), someone solid but alive, someone dignified and noble? A list of characteristics of a fantasy, which the circus supplies, in the living real form of the elephant Anna May, just when you need her most.

Commonplace statements about circus usually include something about a world of fantasy. The ability to lose oneself in this world, which is usually equated with unreality, is often described as something childlike, and the adult experience of it is spoken of as a return to the innocence of childhood. There's certainly something to this return-to-childhood idea: witness my friend Vicki's husband, Robert, who turned to her after an evening at The Big Apple Circus and remarked, "Now I know *exactly* what you were like when you were seven years old." But it wasn't a mist of unreality or innocence or unknowingness he was looking at, but a knowing, excited, tranced, wild child, which is another thing entirely. Perhaps part of the process of becoming an adult is learning to shield ourselves from how much we really saw and felt and knew when we were children. One might say that for children the world is ultrareal, until they outgrow it. Arguably, both the terror and pleasure of being a human animal are most vivid, and all intermingled, when the experience is most new, and possibly this is the supposed "return to childhood" that the circus provides for adults: a return to reality and its origins.

I should confess, here, to a personal prejudice in favor of four-year-olds, or the ones of my acquaintance, anyway, who were all of them interested, more than anything else, in matters of life, death, love, sex, time, danger, trust, God, and how things work. Circus presents a ritual through which these same wonders and risks may be explored and navigated, and it seems to me bizarre to suppose that this is solely children's territory, when this is where we are all the days of our lives, though we may learn, as we grow, not to know it. In fact, circus is intolerable for some very young children; it may be they know too much about it. I have seen toddlers absolutely terrified at the sight, so nearby, of an elephant. They *know* elephants are big.

This turns out to be the first and most important thing to know about elephants, and it's interesting to discover how few adults realize this fact, and how little they respect it. It took me a few days of going along for a walk with two baby elephants at The Circus Knie to understand this myself. In many ways they were similar to puppies, and walking with them involved their handler in many of the same charms and difficulties as strolling with puppies; but each of these puppies was the size of a mini-van, and that made a big difference. I also learned a little about what it means that an animal has a trunk, something most of us aren't used to. And these were very *little* elephants, mind you. No pictures or movies or books had prepared me for all this, though they may have insulated me. The frightened two- or three-year-old hasn't been insulated yet—so she knows.

I haven't anything against art or literature, mind you; I am only intrigued, and often bothered, by the way our theories, abstractions, and images of other animals, devised in the witty labyrinths of our minds, form elaborate barriers between us and them. It's so interesting to build these intricate structures that we forget how much they shut out. It becomes hard to think what the right way of talking about animals might be. For example, here comes a person with a theory about an animal; let's say it concerns an elephant. She dances off with what she thinks is an elephant, all elephants with a capital *E*, in a spirited waltz of equality, empathy, knowledge, and love. But really she's doing a weird solo out there. She thinks she has a partner, but the empty space her arms reach around is occupied by an abstraction. I sympathize, because for a human being this may be the most practical, the safest way to proceed, a real elephant being much too big and sapient to dance with in this fashion. You have to dance with a real elephant *her* way, and that means you have to be willing to do the hard work of learning a whole new way of dancing. This is why people who live and work with animals talk about animals in ways very different from the rest of us, and why I wish they were more widely listened to.

Some years after the Thousand and One Nights show, this same Vanessa Thomas, who had plunged from the top of the tent onto Anna May's back, performed an extended *pas de deux* with Anna May in another show at The Big Apple Circus. For all Vanessa's circus experience, she had never performed a long, complex act with an elephant before. Anna May, however, was an old hand at it. She came to this country from India in 1949 and has been part of the Woodcock family ever since. Her first human partner was William Woodcock, who named her in honor of the movie star Anna May Wong. His son Bill, known as Buckles, has been with her since he was fourteen years old; *his* son,

Ben Williams, grew up with her. Now, at age forty-nine, Anna May is world famous, remarkable for her skills as a dancer, acrobat, and all-round performer. When I went to visit The Circus Knie in Switzerland, with a letter of introduction from The Big Apple Circus, the first thing Louis Knie said to me, as he shook my hand, was, "You come from New York? How is Anna May?"

Now, Vanessa doesn't train elephants; that's Bill Woodcock's job. But she works twice a day with—and atop, under, spun through the air by—not "elephants," but one real and particular elephant, the best in the business. Listening to Vanessa talk about this, I realize all over again that I can't speak with validity about elephants because I've never worked with one, and it's not a rhetoric you can invent at second hand.

Let's drop this nonsense about "equal partnership" here, because Anna May is the superior, the one who knows what she's doing and how it ought to be done. Vanessa is the neophyte, and Anna May lets her know it. A newcomer called to sing a duet with Marilyn Horne does not go on about equality. Vanessa shakes her head and says, "Anna May keeps saying, 'Who's this woman Vanessa? She's not Buckles or Ben or the kids. Oh, all right, here we go again, to teach another person what's what. But I must say, this one is really a *klutz*.'

"Maybe I've had a hamburger or two for dinner. And when she lifts me up with her trunk, she grunts and she *groans*. Buckles is saying, 'Anna May, trunk up!' and she lifts me up, but so *sloooowly* — I mean, really! She weighs 8,000 pounds! But she still lets me know, with her trunk — she might even give me a little pat down here — 'I must say you're getting kind of a pot belly down here, honey.'

"It's so hard to learn what to do, what not to do. It's not always what you might think. When I was learning the mount, Buckles said, 'Put your foot here, right above her eye. There's a boney ledge there and it won't bother her.' I'm saying, 'I can't do that! I might hurt her!' and Anna May's saying, 'What's the delay here? Will somebody *please* get this woman *moving*?' and finally Buckles says, 'Look, put your foot there, Vanessa, she *expects* you to put your foot there,' and I do, and Anna May says, 'Well, *finally*!'

"She can make you feel real stupid that way. One time someone took a photograph of me sitting on her, and when I saw it, I realized I'd let my dress hang down right over her eyes so that she simply couldn't see a thing. I'd been totally oblivious to what I was doing, but she didn't fuss about it. She's much too professional to do that. She knows I'm incompetent and she must think, '*When* is this woman going to get her act together?' But she's totally professional about it.

"Really, she knows so much more about what we're doing than I do, that's the truth. And I don't think she'll *ever* let me forget it." Vanessa laughs, shakes her head again. "I tell you. Anna May is — really —*something*."

This is not an abstract elephant Vanessa is telling about, or a representative or quantified or an absolute elephant, or an elephant in hiding. She's Anna May: one particular elephant with a name, a personality, experience, knowledge, skills, and strong opinions. She's so wonderfully large, and so outside our usual ken, that she's a prime target on which to fasten the categories, moral judgments, and other generalizations with which we try to keep ourselves from getting dizzy and lost in the world. But it's helpful to have her right before us to remind us that she exists.

She's real, and at the circus we have the chance to know what's real, over and over again. We need fantasies,

and circus acknowledges that fantasy is reality wildly elaborated, reality in focus.

Take families, for instance. The Tangier Troupe, next to explode into the ring, consists of eight incredibly strong and supple men who tumble and who also build human pyramids. The word *troupe* strikes me as lovely, resonating of tribe, herd, and family; and, watching them, I sense resemblances to support this fantasy, if you will, of family. Each member of the troupe is unique and skilled on his own, but each one calls our attention to the next one in turn, summoning up our admiration of his brother. When they begin lightly springing up on one another's knees, one hoisting another with adroitly clasped hands onto dependably strong shoulders, you think, That's more than teamwork, that's family solidarity. They demonstrate, in one complex pyramid after another, in a number of curious ways — each of which makes perfect sense, because it works — the whole grand idea of balancing a family, of having it cohere and not fall apart. Each person's strength sustains the whole.

One by one, the members of this family climb up to form an inverted pyramid, a structure of tension and counterbalance. The last two men who join this pyramid are not on its central axis but attach themselves, at the last minute — exiguously, briefly, but there they are — to the sides. At this one point, a single man — he doesn't look particularly large — supports the weight of the whole group, more than a thousand pounds. They are all straining, but also smiling. The center holds. Then the whole thing disassembles; it doesn't fall apart, that would be dangerous, and there's nothing disorganized about the exactitude with which each fellow springs down to gain his own feet again.

As adults, we barely believe that this is possible. One person said to me later, "It shouldn't be possible, but somehow they did it." This is not a response to simple weight lifting. It recognizes the perils of supporting live weight, the weight of personalities. I wonder whether this feat would be quite so wonderfully barely credible, if we had not each felt, way back when, the profoundest fear of being let fall, of being deserted, let down, by our nearest and dearest, and then had not, to some extent, forgotten about it. Why else would this exaggerated fantasy of family solidarity seem so delicious, especially when the pattern dissolves in a bright torrent of leaping, somersaulting bodies to the ground, from which they spring up together, alive, well, and joyous?

The Moroccans make flipping look easy. They take turns zooming around the ring, making the circuit in more ways than you can imagine of using the ground as a springboard. This is a family that lets each person shine on his own, too, each one extravagantly miming, with his whole body, Now! Look at me! Not him! ME!

You do a series of doubletakes, trying to comprehend that their rapid-fire flipping bodies are human, aware all the time that they clearly are. The beauty of circus draws us into the conviction that our species is endlessly beautiful and limitless in its possibilities. Paul Binder has said that you wouldn't recognize any of these people if they were to sit next to you at a lunch counter. Once I ran into the Moroccans beside Lake Champlain, where they'd gone for a swim between shows on a hot afternoon. The sight of those bodies in bathing suits, as they practiced handstands, backflips, and pyramids, to the wonderment of the people from Burlington sharing the beach with them, made me go back and argue with Paul on this point. And of course he pointed out that the beach isn't a lunch counter.

He's right in the implication that daily life, life at lunch counters, clothed life, isn't art, and circus people are artists. But they are human — creaturely. It happens that they are artists of the body, and the beginning of our wonder is the beauty of their bodies. But our response doesn't stop with awe and admiration, which, I think, carry within them a kind of uneasiness, an "I could never look like that." I could never look like someone in *Vogue*. Not only could I never dance like Makarova, but who could? She could hardly be human, and must belong to some other, more rarified species entirely. Circus, however, involves a quite opposite aesthetic. Circus people take risks with their beauty, pushing it to extremes of danger, distortion, ridiculousness, and impossibility. They also radiate pleasure in their own selves. During her belly dance, Vanessa reacts to the wolf whistles from the audience with a complicitous, sparkling grin. To all of this, you are apt to respond with an expanded awareness of what it is to be human, and fully alive in your own body, whatever its dimensions. You're helped in this by the ring and your part in it, which not only allows but encourages in you a total physical response. Your hands, heart, lungs, nerves, voice get a good workout, your feet, too, if you're a stamper. Circus people involve you in their effort, regardless of who you assume you are.

The show is characterized by magical disappearances and appearances and by startling shifts of mood, the lighting running the spectrum from the glare of midday to mysterious blue moonlight, the music changing with it. There are kaleidoscope tumbles from one species to another. You stop thinking of animals on one hand, people on the other. It turns out that there are a lot more different kinds of people than you are used to thinking of, but that's just the beginning; it turns out there are myriad ways of living and moving in a human body. It turns out that some of us can turn inside out or use the ground as a temporary touch-point for flipping around above it. It turns out that some of us can fly. It never stops being startling, just as, perhaps, there are days when it's startling, sometimes in an exuberant way, sometimes in an awful way, to live in a body, yourself. But in this show, whose very theme is the bizarre quality of life when looked at closely, ordinary barriers, barriers which are both frustrating and comforting — barriers within ourselves, between different people, between our kind and other animals — blur and flicker.

I want to tell you about the genie in the lamp. The genie in the original story is one terrifying creature. When Aladdin summons him, it is an experience of the sublime. The genie emerges from a tiny lamp, he is huge, he fills the air. He's been in the lamp for a great many years and *he wants out*. Now, in The Big Apple Circus, the genie is one Hugo Zamoratte. He was born in Tucumán, Argentina. "He was working as an accountant at the Ministry of Foreign Affairs," the program says, "when he decided to go to gymnastic school, at the age of twenty. There, he discovered that he could extend and maneuver his body into almost any desired position. For the next six years, he went on practicing, preparing his body and mind to perform by studying yoga at the same time. . . ."

The Big Apple Circus program is full of stories of metamorphoses such as this one. It abounds with accounts of concentration and transformation. "Hassan Ousrout, the leader of the Tangier Troupe, started learning his craft at the age of eleven, under the guidance of his uncle, who himself was the fourth generation of a family of Moroccan acrobats. . . ." "Dolly Jacobs started her career as a showgirl with Ringling Brothers, Barnum & Bailey Circus, where her father, the celebrated clown, Lou Jacobs, had been a featured artist for more than sixty years. When she decided to follow in her mother's footsteps as an aerealist, her godmother, Martie Geiger, helped her to create the wonderful Roman Rings act that made her the undisputed Queen of the Air. . . ." "Born in Petit-Lancy, Switzerland, of an American father and a Swiss mother, Mireille Fenwick completed advanced studies in Latin, before making her childhood dream come true by joining the Conservatoire National des Arts du Cirque in Paris, in 1977. There, she met Guillaume Dufresnoy, a young mathematician from Bordeaux, France, who abandoned a promising career as an engineer to join the circus. . . ." "Katja Schumann was born into one of the world's oldest and most celebrated equestrian circus families. The Circus Schumann, founded in 1870, was established in Denmark in 1891, where the name Schumann has since become synonymous with Circus. The daughter of the famous *maître-écuyer* Max Schumann, Katja made her first appearance in the ring at the age of ten. After having performed various *haute école*, Liberty, and bareback riding acts, Katja made circus history in 1985 as the first woman to perform a complete version of 'The Courier' in America. . . ." "Marie-Pierre Benac, while studying design at Paris University, joined Alexis Gruss' circus school as a means of keeping in shape. Mr. Gruss was quick to recognize her potential and invited her to join the

French National Circus company. . . . She joined The
Big Apple Circus in 1984, where she performed on tightwire, horseback, with elephants, on rotating trapeze, and
on the Russian Barre, her trademark act. . . ." "When not
on tour with the circus, Michael Christensen (Mr. Stubs)
supervises The Big Apple Circus' Clown Care Unit,
which visits young patients in New York City's Presby-
terian and St. Luke's–Roosevelt Hospitals. . . ." "Paul
Binder . . . graduated from Dartmouth College, earned
an M.B.A. at Columbia University . . . and headed to San
Francisco, to juggle. . . . Before long, Paul and Michael
Christensen were travelling throughout Europe, earning
their living juggling on street corners. . . . They were discovered by Annie Fratellini and Pierre Étaix, who invited
them to join their Nouveau Cirque de Paris. . . . By mar-
rying Danish equestrienne Katja Schumann, Paul joined
circus aristocracy, and he and Katja have started a new
circus lineage with their children, Katherine Rose and
Max Abraham. . . ."

I love the way these people explain who they are. It is a
catalogue of intensities. In America, people usually ask
someone they don't know, "What do you do?" and they
usually want to know precisely that, so that the unknown

can quickly be categorized and satisfactorily put in a slot. But circus people seem to value wonderfully, by their descriptions of themselves, a whole different set of questions, such as, Who are you? Where are you from? What is your clan, your country, your tradition? Where have you been, who are your teachers? What do you love? What fantasy are you dedicating yourself to? It is another way in which circus makes expectable boundaries tremble like mirages. You see possibilities, not limits.

"What do you do?"

"Well, I'm a contortionist." Or —

"I'm working on being the bottom of a human pyramid and I'm trying to figure out all the ways there might be of holding up seven other guys in midair." Or —

"I'm learning how to do arabesques, *en pointe*, on the tightwire." Or —

"Well, right now I'm training a group of horses to jump through hoops, and some of them are learning how to break through paper-covered hoops, and eventually I might train one of them who shows a talent for it to jump over another horse. . . ."

Why not? I start to wonder, why not do the important thing, whatever that may be? — since within this ring anything is possible, anything (no matter how obscure or singular or strange it may sound outside this circle) is important. Work is what you love and do completely. They make this make perfect sense.

So. His face serious and remote, Mr. Stubs elevates the lamp above his head as if he were a priest. He rubs the lamp, holding it over an ominous rug-covered shape. The rug is ceremoniously swept away, and in a darkened ring, lit by one spotlight only, is a transparent, gold-glowing box, on a table. It isn't big, perhaps a yard high, a couple of feet wide. There is something in it, pressed and curled inside. A hand appears out the top, then a wrist, the sharp angle of a shoulder. The audience gasps in a wave. *There is a man in there*.

This is Zamoratte, the contortionist, emerging. When he is out of the box, he works atop the table, clad in flowing oriental trousers and a jeweled cap. His torso is bare; his face wears an otherworldly smile. He has a tall, muscular body, with long, sinewy arms, long legs, and elegant, powerfully arched feet. For a few moments, standing upright in display, he asserts his perfection, as if to say, Remember, I am beautiful, not grotesque. Then, standing, sitting, or lying down, in movements of sinuous

grace, he quite literally ties himself into knots. His legs, both of them, disappear behind his neck; he is there only from the bottom up, as if he had no legs at all. It is the worst dream of amputation, and yet he's fine, even wonderful. He does the same thing with his arms, seeming to unjoint them and lose them behind, beneath himself. Awfully, he seems to come apart: he is a person who has hands like flippers, but no arms; then, there they are again. Deformity turns out to be a false, if terrifying, category. Sometimes his expression turns disingenuous, as if he's as surprised by his dislocating joints as we are. But for the most part, his constant smile is quite detached.

Watching Zamoratte, the spectator is robbed, by sleight-of-body, of the familiar bodily checkpoints — no more front and back, top and bottom. But as he disentangles, over and over, you begin to realize that it's all the same man, with variations on that theme played in tones of dreamy intensity. It's not the resolution of the distortions that allays anxiety; it is the unshockable expression of the subject, his concentration on, and appreciation of, his own oddities — that is, his bodily confidence; his grace.

Finally, his slaves, the clowns, appear with a transparent bottle. It is incredibly small, a bell jar with a tiny door on one side. Slowly, slowly, beginning with his feet, he undoes his joints, turning, rearranging all parts of himself and pouring himself, bit by bit, through the tiny door into the bottle. I glance at my neighbor and feel that she shares — or I badly need a sense of corroboration in this — my feeling that I wish he would stop. It is too much, too awful. The murmuring of the audience is almost anguished. And yet, after that glance, we both swing our eyes back to that bottle, because we can't stop watching him, the disassembling man, the man freely, carefully, intricately engaging in the worst nightmare of entering the too-small space.

You will have to take my word for it: he gets himself totally inside. A golden light illuminates the bottle as Mr. Stubs swings the little door shut, and the bottle, with its golden contents, his skin pressed against every bit of the glass surface from within, no gaps or spaces visible anywhere, slowly revolves. I think, The womb is transparent, the fetus is glowing in the bottle — out, I want him *out* — and then, when I can barely stand it any longer, the door is opened, and — oh God, a hand — it waves. And slowly, slowly, he emerges, a shoulderblade protruding oddly, then reassembling as a shoulder, a leg back from beyond reaffirms itself as a leg. Before us the genie reconstructs himself and emerges. The claustrophobic nightmare is resolved. Climbing to his feet, he stretches to embrace space in all directions. He's free! Smiling, to waves of music, he sweeps great bows. Still, I feel shaken, stunned.

And in comes Gordoon the clown. Again — just when we need it — the right creature.

Gordoon has a white face with red dots of cheeks and a bulbous shiny red nose; he wears a checkered swimming cap on his head, a floppy red-and-white-striped nightgown/bathing dress down to his knees, then black-and-white striped tights which end at spats and clumpy black lace-up boots. Sometimes a black frock coat and a red derby top it all off. It's a manic conglomeration of antiquated components that bring to mind an old, too-brightly-colored postcard showing someone acting very silly on the beach at a cheap late-Victorian seaside resort. He is bouncy and guileless as a puppy, given to outbursts of uncontrollable happiness: an optimist, pure and simple.

Gordoon appears to be sitting on a skirted table which is carried in by his clown friends, Mr. Stubs, Mr. Fish, and Oaf, to music which has suddenly assumed the merry cadences of a hoedown. Now Gordoon starts doing very funny things with what may or may not be his feet — twiddles them, bends them backward in hairpin turns, spins them in impossible 360-degree circles. At this point Mr. Paul appears to one side, folds his arms, cocks his head, and stares, regarding the spectacle with frowning, but resigned, skepticism. Pretty soon he shakes his head and simply throws up his hands, making a quick exit. Now Gordoon fools around with his extremely peculiar legs. Ties them in knots. Double, triple knots! Then his feet fly right off. He crows with delight at the sight of his flying

feet. Then Mr. Fish and Oaf grab his legs, plunge sideways with them, so that they're stretched out to become
ten feet long. Gordoon whoops, "Wheeee!"

Now, I don't know about you, but I feel a lot better,
laughing about that. Even though for a moment, at the beginning (and even allowing for my gullible nature, I still
don't think I'm alone in this), I needed to tell myself, Oh,
whew, I bet those aren't really his legs. Which was exactly
what I longed to say about the genie's legs. But I wasn't
allowed.

This experience with the genie, beginning ominously,
proceeding through permutations of fear, beauty, and
awe, and finishing with release and then hilarity, is absolutely one of circus. Creaturely lines are blurred, and animal life — one's own life, in this case, in a body — is explored and heightened. If I say that children know more
about extremes than does the average sane adult, I am re-
marking on averages in a very average view of our culture, so perhaps "child" and "adult" are false labels. It
would be wiser, perhaps, to say that some people are more
aware than others of the need to go to the edge, or to push
toward it, and of the pleasures of the return from that
edge. This has nothing to do with innocence or belief in

make-believe, but with awareness, with both the delight and the pain inherent in complete consciousness.

This show is patterned, to an extent that deprives us all of our thick skins, on this play of unsettling — or magical, if you will — extremes. It says, *normal* is a stupid word; it means nothing. The oddity of atmosphere allows the performers to take the risk of exploring creaturely themes, and to take us with them.

Circus blurs distinctions between people and animals in the manner of myths, and the potency of myths derives from their play, not at the edges of reality, but at its live center. Circus artists, human and other, are full of magic and surrounded by it, but their art is one of distilled essence of reality, including all of God's creation. When the circus horses appear, they embody the distilled, vivid essence of Horse. You can hear them, smell them, almost stroke their glossy necks and haunches. They are *all there*. But because of the beauty of their performance, they are at once the mythical horses who let people metamorphose into centaurs. They are no less real than a vivid and well-informed dream of horses is real, no less than a rider's aim of becoming as one with his horse is real.

Something happens to the audience whenever circus

horses enter the ring. There's a stillness, swift as a sudden intake of breath; the light alters, something shines in the air. The appearance of any creature changes the weather: the camels bring hilarity with them, and the great elephants knock everyone silly with joy. But the horses carry wonder in with them. I can't explain why this is so. But it happens, every time.

Horses, I think, now horses are something I know something about (as opposed, say, to genies in bottles). Nonetheless, throughout the Liberty act, I keep thinking, I can't believe this; can you believe that? I am reminded of the story about Margaret Fuller walking along with Ralph Waldo Emerson, and walking full tilt into a tree. "Why, Margaret," Emerson says, helping her to her feet, "didn't you see that tree?" And she replies, perhaps crossly, but I prefer to think speculatively, "Yes, certainly I *saw* it, but I didn't *realize* it."

Katja Schumann, the trainer of the circus horses, is also our Scheherazade, and so by this time we recognize her willowy bejeweled figure, her flowing hair and harem pants, and the clarity with which her vivid face and body express whatever she has in mind. But when she takes to the center of the ring, with her horses around her, the character and her genius suddenly make complete sense. Scheherazade is a horsewoman.

There are two chestnut stallions, Khan and Said, whose bodies, manes, and tails are all of a rich deep red; two palominos, Basha and Temudschin, creamy gold with flaxen manes and tails; and two pale grays, Taif and Arabi, whose manes and tails are silver. Like mythic horses of the desert, they wear tasseled halters, and necklaces of long scarlet fringe hang at their breasts, swaying

with their every move. The six stallions trot around the ring in procession, in single file, in pairs, and in threes, changing direction in lively pirouettes. Wheeling six abreast, they fill the whole ring with their patterns. Forward, always forward, they burst into a gallop, heads tossing, manes and tails windborne, changing direction with flying leaps and moving adroitly in intricate formations.

Scheherazade conducts this dance by dancing, her whole body moving forward and back in rapid steps or slow, regal swings. She speaks to the horses by name, below the music, in tones modulated for them alone. In each hand she holds a light whip, and she gestures with them like a conductor with two batons. When she lifts her arms from her sides and steps forward, lifting her whole body up from the center, the stallions before her rise up rearing, balancing above her on their hind legs. They proceed to the edge of the ring and, facing the audience, put their front hooves carefully up on the ring curb, balancing there, necks arched, looming over the people in the first few rows in a stance of perfect stillness. Then, seemingly unbidden, called in a way that only they can comprehend, they fly off again.

The horses do Katja Schumann's bidding "at liberty," their free wills willingly engaged in hers; that is, she and her horses share a deep and focused set of intentions. It is not her command of them, nor their obedience to her, that makes it look easy; their aesthetic transcends these mechanical stereotypes. What stuns us so joyously is the clear play of their mutual intention, which combines intensity and ease.

This matter of "making it look easy" crops up over and over again in circus, as, I suppose, in all art. As I have said, in circus this impression of effortlessness is complicated and enriched by the glimpses we are allowed of real effort and immediate risk, and by the vast array of sense impressions available to us because of our intimacy with the ring. Anyone who knows anything about horses knows, moreover, that what Katja does with her horses isn't easy, nor is it easily arrived at; and it worries me that if you are unfamiliar with horses yourself, you may not know what I'm talking about. In days not so long gone by, almost everyone had contact with horses, one way or another (and with other sorts of big animals, too), day in, day out. The rhythms of horses' feet — *1234, 1234, 1234* (walking); *1, 2, 1, 2, 1, 2,* (spondees steadily marching at the trot); and

123–, 123–, 123–(the swing of the canter with its waltzing moment of suspension)—were everywhere, an unremarkable attribute of the world, a source of music as ubiquitous as the human heartbeat. People were close to the sight and smell and touch of horses. For most of us, this is no longer true, and no photograph, no movie, and—yes—no book can duplicate horses with you in the here and now. Honesty, and the presence of horses, compel me to warn you about this. I once asked Katja whether it has ever bothered her that the complicated work she does with her horses may not be recognized or appreciated. "My father," she replied, "who was my good teacher, used to say to me, 'Don't despair. There's always one person out there who knows what you're doing. *He paid for his ticket.* So you're all right.'"

In the empty tent in the mornings, the training sessions proceed. What she and the horses do together is endless, endless, careful, subtle work. The atmosphere is one of orderly quiet, focused by her moving body, her low, crooning voice, her deep concentration, and her imperturbable willingness to move unhurriedly sideways in time. The work places high demands on her own and her horses' perception and intelligence, equally. She literally

lives with them. For months on the road she can hear every shuffle of every hoof in the portable stalls under the stable-tent, set up always as close as can be to the front door of the trailer which is her home. The great horseman William Steinkraus, in a film about equestrian Olympic sports, was asked for his evaluation of the intelligence of horses, and he replied that it's hard to know, but that we probably greatly underestimate their intelligence because we don't live with them, the way we do with dogs. But these horses and this trainer do live together, side by side, in constant sight, sound, and smell of each other, and they all work together for hours, day after day. She and they are almost palpably attuned to each other, in an endless loop of communication. This is not only not easy — it seldom happens, between people and horses — but it is the essence of the process called training, and of circus training in particular. But Katja would say — has said, in fact — that what she does is very simple. Their work has all the refinement of simplicity endlessly elaborated. From that carefully built, solid foundation, they spring into the ring, and own it. If we say it looks easy, we mean it in the way one might say, When I dreamed of flying, it was — easy.

What some people find passionately interesting about horses, other people fear: their combined size and sensitivity; the sense of a consciousness both heightened and remote; what the old books used to call their "excitability to motion." When I say, Some people are afraid of horses, I am not speaking of an attitude of sensible respect, or of informed, cautionary awe, both of which are proper to the task of knowing horses. I mean the anxiety at being in the presence of power which it seems impossible to interpret. If you are familiar with this sort of trepidation, you may well find the Liberty horses particularly interesting because they give you the opportunity to figure it out, if you pay attention. They take over: they flash past; their hooves pound; they snort, wheel, rear. But the horses are both free and encircled, dancing with the beautiful woman in the ring specially formed as their dance floor. Like everyone else who enters that ring, she and they together are artists, and they know what they are doing.

Katja's work with her horses is completely free of the bizarre ways in which fearful people imagine that power must be dealt with: that is, with force and domination, on the one hand, or, on the other, with bribery, cajolery, and corruption. Where there's no knowledge, symbolism goes crazy. The truth of the matter is that neither violence nor its other face, which is sentimentality, will get you anywhere with a horse. Instead, both horses and trainer are under the control of an art form which has risen, over centuries, from close observation of, and careful thinking about, how horses function and who they are. The art of horsemanship is not improvisatory, but formal, and what's going on in the ring is so subtle that we may not be able to recognize the details, so quickly do they fly by.

Something I read in the "Q. & A." column in the Science section of the *New York Times* has to do with our perception of other creatures. A reader wrote to ask: "Why do butterflies flit aimlessly, in a random path from point to point?" The answer, provided by Dr. Louis Sorkin, an entomologist at the American Museum of Natural History, began with: "It looks like flitting, but you're not a butterfly." After proposing a number of possible crucial motivations for a butterfly's apparently random movements, he concluded that because a butterfly, unlike a bee, does not live in a colony, "There is no reason to fly in a straight line from point to point. . . . It is not going home. There is no home."

In the presence of any animal, one might do well to

keep this lovely summary of meanings in mind. I like to think of Dr. Sorkin sitting, perhaps, on the grass, near some flowers interesting to butterflies, in the bright afternoon sun, observing them fastidiously. He knows his details. And yet he's not afraid to put what has been called the most beautiful word in the English language — *home* — at the numinous heart of his interpretations. He is proceeding just as Thoreau says one must: "To appreciate a single phenomenon . . . you must camp down here beside it as if for life . . . and give yourself utterly to it. It must stand for the whole world to you, and be symbolical of all things" (*Journal*, December 1853). This is the only way to think about an animal that makes any sense, and it's also the way that good circus trainers think, every day of their lives with animals. The animals and people in the ring also offer the spectator a position — "camped down here beside it as if for life" — from which to see that there are things to know about them that are really true.

You have to give up hallucinations: "*It is not going home. There is no home.*" In their place, you have the horses and their trainer showing that knowledge and art give form to power. They say that animals and people can safely, beautifully take the risks of creating that form together. They replace brutal and sentimental falsehoods with the death-less fantasy of authentic and mutual creative empower-ment. And, because we're at the circus, that fantasy comes true.

Now all the horses except Temudschin and Khan have left the ring, and the palomino and chestnut gallop side by side, white gold and red gold. Scheherazade, running, takes to the circle herself, meets them head-on, and slips between them, as they part slightly to let her pass between their gleaming bodies, past their flying feet. She smiles, and dashes to meet them again. This time they form a trio, all running in the same direction. She seizes hold of Te-mudschin's surcingle, so that his stride lifts and impels hers. Then, using the ground and his momentum as a springboard, she vaults onto his back. The three of them sweep once around together, then wheel at the top of the ring, gallop down it, and, leaping over a banqueting table where the clowns have come carousing in front of the open curtain, they disappear from sight.

At this dashing flourish of an exit, there is, in the au-dience, a wave of longing and regret. The eruption of ap-plause and cheering has in it a plangent cry: More, we want more! DON'T GO!

So there is something to be learned, or reminded of, about endings, too — which are only interruptions, really, when we speak of knowledge, and of dreams.

But this is the circus, so we simply pass into another. The stilt dancers, Jim and Tisha Tinsman, are an elegantly clad couple, veiled and spangled, a sort of oriental fairy-tale version of Fred Astaire and Ginger Rogers swooping and gliding together. The crazy difference is that they are about twelve feet tall. Their torsos are of normal proportions but — so much, again, for normal — their legs go on forever. Their dance is another kind of distortion, ungainly and graceful, wonderful but disturbing. They twirl and balance in stylish measures; at one point he supports her in a perfect arabesque, which is not a parody at all, though the extended leg looks endless. Her legs, in fact, end in ballet shoes; she dances *en pointe*. Altered height and courtly forms play off each other with elegance and dash as the bright costumes shimmer and sway and the charming faces smile, miles up. Where do these two leave off being human, as we understand the term?

The stilt dancers are the most *clothed* people we'll see tonight, among the acrobats and dancers. They have the

most to cover up! I'm usually curious about the processes behind performance; I want secret ingenuities to come out of hiding. But in this case, even mulling it over long after the fact, I find myself uninspired to wonder what the stilts really look like, under those costumes, how they're fastened, how they're managed. In this case I'm quite content to have what's hidden remain hidden. The impression that the dancers feel all of a piece is so complete that I have no wish to dissect them. Only now do I realize, for example, that they weren't holding on to anything; their hands clutched at no supports, their arms were free to gesture. There were no awkward, clunky angles on their legs, and no stumping effect as they stepped. None of this occurred to me at the time. The cover-up was completely convincing.

We're witnessing a dream — it could be delightful, or funny, or a nightmare, or all three — of being unbelievably tall but unusually mobile. In this extreme state one can imagine functioning in a different realm of space, as in a successful reverie about possessing seven-league boots. If you've ever been immobilized in some major way, you know that walking is like a dream. I remember lying in a hospital bed with a broken femur, watching people hurry past the open door with what seemed to me insouciance beyond all comprehending; they possessed a supernatural skill and didn't even know it. It wasn't envy that caused me to have the door closed; I just couldn't stand the pressure of my own amazement. Dreams come to modern people as a series of questions, nagging for interpretation. Here in the ring (which is not a modern place), dreams are answers, complete in themselves, free from explication. What matters with the stilt dancers is the weird, lovely play of effortless grace with impossible dimensions. It's unusual, but a fact, that one doesn't feel a need to know the how and why of them.

If being human means you can dance expressively with six-extra-feet-long legs, it also means, it turns out, that you can fly. In fact, aerialists such as Les Casalys are often referred to as flyers. Mireille and Guillaume perform an aerial act in which Guillaume *is* the trapeze. He sits at the top of the tent on a special perch which allows him to drop over backward and hang by his knees. His lower legs are horizontal and stable, anchored by strength, but the rest of him, from his pivoting knees on, swings back and forth like a pendulum. His arms outstretched, he catches Mireille with his hands as she leaps from beside or above him

on the platform, and, their hands locked, he swings her back and forth, in great, bending arcs that begin with his knees and go through his extended body, then hers, and end with her pointed toes.

Guillaume is a tall, elegant man, with a long bare torso, discreetly but definitively ridged, and broad, bony shoulders. He's one of those men who seem made of a peculiarly supple kind of wood, each joining clearly articulated, and the grain showing. His legs, in their white tights, seem to go on forever. Mireille stands very close to him, and just above him, between flights, in the position from which she dives into the air so that he can fall back, reach out to catch and swing her. She's a tiny woman, but she doesn't look sylphlike; she seems to be composed of perfect and compact curves. They look great together, and they seem to know it, although their demeanor is completely free of arrogance. They confide the happy fact that it's lovely to be human. His lean face breaks into a boyish grin, crinkly around the eyes and endlessly knowledgeable. A thin jeweled band encircles her cap of dark curly hair, and there are spangles, too, on her minute white leotard, but she exudes a pretty freshness rather than glamour. They are like best friends who feel lucky to be together, who say, without speech, Leap, and I'll catch you! and, When you reach for me, my hands will find yours. The wide arm gestures with which they acknowledge applause between movements look like the sort of greeting an old friend might give you, right before the hug.

This act involves a complicated rigging of bars and ropes, deep concentration, profound technical expertise, and intensities of timing and strength which we can only guess at, as they swing, flip, dive, and catch hold so far above us. I have seen this act several times, and I can tell you all about the limits of fear and trust it takes us to, but I am certain that if I were to see it again tomorrow, these feelings would arise as if for the first time. There's nothing routine about it, for either performers or spectators; each time is the first time. When the audience isn't cheering, it is breathlessly silent, gazing up. I always fear that the weight of all those souls, born upward to the flyers in the air, might be too great for them to bear.

This particular night, I am struck by the slow, deliberate way in which Les Casalys chalk their hands and wrists. This activity creates pauses in the act, like commas in a sentence, or caesuras in verse. The perfect man and woman in their sleek white leotards turn their hands and wrists over and over, rubbing on the chalk. Their smiles and gestures are warm and confiding, throughout this mundane powdering, and there's no attempt to divert our attention from it, because it's a natural part of the technique. It's as if they were saying, We're not going to hide the risk from you, nor the exactness with which we control the risk. What we are doing is not make-believe. Flying is real. (The one-ring circus is the home of this kind of concentration. The three-ring extravaganza destroys this focus, diffusing attention away from the details.) Then I thought — not because of any hint of strain in them, or any tinge of anguish, but only because of the intensity of their engagement in this technicality — how hot it must be, at the top of the tent. Indeed, in the course of a summer of record-breaking heat, the top of the tent went well over 100 degrees during many a matinee. So I learn a lot, in a short time, about what it entails for a person to fly.

Circus is said to center on tricks. A funny word, implying something factitious, manipulative, insincere. Something to watch out for, be on your guard against. Circus lures people out of isolation and into the stunning details of life, and I suppose some might insist that the only way anyone is going to do this is by tricking them into it. To the contrary, I believe that if what we saw in the ring, and above it, were false, we wouldn't believe it, and what we experience around that ring is belief. Lies would be as out of place here as they would be in authentic religious ritual.

Paul Binder's program notes explain the matter this way: "We measure performers at The Big Apple Circus by two very strict standards: their technical excellence, and the ability to communicate emotional involvement in the presentation, their contact with the audience. The resulting effect is a series of 'virtuoso moments' (don't call them *tricks*). . . ."

In the mythology of flying, there usually is a trick involved. The story of Daedalus and Icarus is about a trick—ingenious technology—that didn't work. If you literally fly in the face of gravity and the sun's energy, death will find you out. To take to the air successfully, you have to be a god or goddess (Hermes dashing about, the Virgin ascending), or you have to turn yourself into a passenger (on Pegasus, on airplane, the space shuttle), or you have to shift shapes (becoming an eagle, or a swan, white or black). Les Casalys remake the mythology. They take to the air, but they are still one (or two) of us — lovelier, more highly trained, perhaps, but absolutely human, subject to the same stresses of gravity, heat, weight, and speed, but dealing with them calmly, cheerfully, high above the ground, and unafraid of letting us see the details. And it works. We gaze up at them as if we've never seen ourselves, our kind, before. All in all, I'm not sure what I think of "virtuoso moments." I turn in the direction of "moments of truth."

In any case, if Mireille and Guillaume were doing tricks, two things would happen: we would not be convinced, and they would fall.

But, of course, we always are, and they never do.

At intermission, you go out, not into a crowded lobby, but into the earthy outdoors on the lot. If it's daytime, you're surprised to find yourself out under the hot sun; at night, the cool darkness hangs right above the circus lights. Hundreds of happy people are milling about the buffets and the souvenir stand. There is an inspiring smell compounded of popcorn, hot dogs, and cotton candy, and be-

hind that, here in the country, you smell green grass. What goes on back here is, naturally, fascinating to circus audiences. In saying that the lives of circus performers represent a dream of freedom and focus, which makes running away to join the circus such a potent idea, I've assumed that what goes on in the ring is no less a true story than what happens outside it. But we'll have a few "outside" stories too, because they have to do with the matter of circus being real life, heightened.

Late one Wednesday night in June 1987, after performing in the matinee and the evening show, Katja Schumann gave birth to Max Abraham Binder in the trailer parked behind the big tent, next to the horse stalls, in the encampment of circus trucks and campers, in Ninety Acres Park in Bridgeport, Connecticut. A summer night like this one.

"I caught him," she told me a couple of days later, "before he hit the floor. He quacked and snorted a little, and I thought, 'This boy looks just fine to me!' so I tucked him in with me under my bathrobe and got into the bed and waited for the midwives to arrive. Paul was with me; it was just as we'd wanted it.

"When the midwives came, I think perhaps they were a little bit flabbergasted by the procession through here. Once the ice was broken, the people in the company were stepping on each other's toes to get in, and those that didn't make it to the bedroom made it to the sink and washed glasses and emptied ashtrays, and everyone gathered and sang 'Happy Birthday' outside. . . .

"At five that afternoon, after the matinee, I had thought to myself, 'Here we go.' Paul is an intense worrier, he can only stand worry for short periods, and he has a lot to worry about during the performance anyway, so I didn't say anything to him. I went into the show without telling anyone. I considered copping out of the riding part" (which included, among other phenomena, jumping her horse at a gallop to burst through a paper-covered hoop), "but it was too short notice, everything would have turned upside down; so I went ahead and rode. I did have a couple of contractions during the act, and I got distracted, befuddled, dropped a hoop, something I've never done before.

"After that, during intermission, Paul and I sat in the dark on the steps out here. And I asked him if he minded if I skipped the finale.

"'Why?' he asked.

"'I've got other things to do!'

"'Are we having a baby tonight?'

"'I think so,' I said.

"So, during the second half of the show Paul was running in and out of here, whenever he wasn't on, and then, of course, when I didn't show up for the finale, everyone in the company knew.

"I didn't know it at the time, but now I think I wasn't doing it just for myself, but for all of us. They all knew my intention, but people aren't used to it. Some avoided the issue, maybe hoped I wouldn't do it this way. People are afraid of being touched. This is strong stuff, you know? But it's brought us together. It brings things out in people they didn't know they had."

That was Wednesday night. On Saturday afternoon, between the matinee and the evening show, Katja, stage makeup still on her face, is nursing Max. His sister, Katherine, who's almost two, bare and round as a little dolphin in the hot humid air, lies with her head on Katja's thigh, watching. "As for myself, I never had any doubt that I was going to do this; the question was how to work out the details. We had great midwives supporting us, and of course we'd already had Katherine, so we knew what was happening." She bends her head to murmur to Katherine in Danish, strokes her curls, then the baby's head, with the light strong hand that can turn six stallions on a dime. "I'm not scared to do what I know, it's as simple as that. But" — her glance over to me is somewhat stern — "I don't want to sound superficial, flippant, about it." (*"Don't call them tricks. . . ."*)

The midwife says, later, "She's right; it would be too bad if everyone thought this was a sensational off-the-wall thing that crazy circus people do. Katja and Paul are intelligent people who rationally chose the intimacy and safety of a home birth. It would also be a pity if this were seen as a trick pulled off by some sort of super-woman, since many women birth this way—have for centuries, still do. It's only very recent American culture that makes it seem so astonishing. Having said all that, I must add that Katja is an extraordinarily centered, self-possessed woman, and her strength comes from a very deep place inside her, or she couldn't have done it the way she did it."

The *way* she did it. It's characteristic of circus artists to make the dangerous and difficult seem possible, to work on intimate terms with realities which many people are busy trying to avoid. Circus goes to the edge, and right to the center. Without the Longhi gown, the palomino and chestnut stallions, without the brilliant smiles and flour-ishes, the artistic play with death and life comes all the way home. Maybe there's a wing's brush of regret at the expansion of a private moment, but her life's work is used to these transformations.

"My grandfather, years ago, asked that when he died, we put his ashes at the foot of an elderflower. They grow everywhere in the countryside in Denmark, you know. And he wanted elderflowers above him. So, when he died, we did that. Well, the other day I noticed that there's an elderberry bush on the edge of the woods behind the trailer, here. I thought, 'That's where I'd like to bury the placenta. . . .'"

Max, a serious sort of person, dressed in his sister's hand-me-down pink booties and a white cotton blanket, gazes up knowledgeably at her voice.

"A funny thing happened at the matinee, yesterday." Katja did take Thursday off, but she was back in the show for Friday's matinee, after her milk came in. "When I'm about to go on for the Venetian Carnivale scene, I'm waiting in this little space behind the curtain. It's very dark back there, stuffy, dusty, very hot. As always, I'm going over a list in my mind to check and see everything's where it belongs — my hat, my mask, my costume's all right, the right shoes. And suddenly I think — 'My God, the baby! *Where's the baby?*' I've become so used to having him with me for every performance, you see. . . .

"So there I was, in a panic, and just then I realized, he's back in the trailer, he's not with me any more. It was really quite lonely, all of a sudden. . . ."

Now it's a year and a couple of months later, and I turn up to watch Katja work her horses one morning in the big deserted tent.

Her grooms have let the stallions into the ring for a few minutes of exercise before the formal work begins. The horses turn themselves inside out in their exuberance, charging, mock-fighting, rearing, wheeling, careening in wild, ebullient play. Then Katja strolls into the ring, calling them quietly to order. Their awareness of her is so acute that they instantly organize their dance into a brisk trotting circle around the ring. In response she croons to them, in French, *"Brave! Brave!"* meaning Good! Nice work! That's fine! In one hand she carries her whip, the light extension of her bidding fingers, the conductor's baton. Over one shoulder is slung a pouch, full of grain which she will offer, in handfuls, to each horse, with a slight, gracious bow, during each pause in the work. Her other arm is wrapped around — Max.

Who is sitting koala style, legs spread around her hip. He's a lovely little boy, tanned to the color of a peach, palest blond hair curling at the tender nape of his neck, his sturdy body completely bare, not a tan line, nor a straight line, on him anywhere. He is all curves, a comfortable, contemplative *putto*. As the horses circle and dash, sawdust flying up from under their hooves, Max regards them with sober concentration, from his turning, dancing perch. One stallion is called to the center of the ring for a handful of grain, and Max reaches out to pat his face, fingers the velvet lips, sticks his chubby hand between them. Basha arches his elegant neck over the baby and, ears pricked forward, lips his fingers, delicately breathes his hair.

So: Max is back with Katja. If you see this scene, you know another piece of the story about the creatures of circus living and working together, their lives all of a piece. You understand how circus depends upon and embodies this wholeness, and the hard work necessary to it.

The Big Apple Circus children live right in among their parents, other adults, one another, and everyone's work; their parents never change into mechanical parts of an abstract world somewhere else. What their parents do all day is no mystery to them. The children attend the One Ring Schoolhouse in a trailer on the lot. At any given time, there may be from eight to twelve children in the school, ranging in ages anywhere from three to eighteen, speaking a variable number of native languages. In the winter of 1991, Lucy Casey, who was at that time the One Ring Schoolhouse's gifted teacher, told me a story:

"One day the school was visiting the library and the librarian said, 'I'm putting on a special program; would you like to come?' It was a film about Thanksgiving, called *The Pilgrim*, and it was about a Russian girl whose parents had just come to America, mainly for religious reasons. She didn't know the language well, there was a lot of prejudice against her, and the other kids were monstrous to her, teased her unmercifully. Well, it took a while, but finally she made a doll the other kids admired, and eventually she made some friends.

"So, here was this earnest movie trying to teach this *message*. But it was so odd for us! *My* kids didn't understand that film at all, they had *no concept*. We're all looking at each other, becoming very, very upset. We were *crying* because of the way the girl was being treated, but my children didn't know *why* she was being treated that way! She didn't sound or look at all different to them — she was totally normal! They were looking and looking at each other — *what's going on?* They had no idea!

"My kids live in this nurturing environment; they've been exposed to all cultures since day one. *Everyone* is family to them. Whenever someone new comes in, they end out being part of the family. Faces change, but it's still family. So they didn't know what this film was about. The librarian must have been quite confused. . . .

"The main thing I notice about these kids, the one thing they have in common, is their *insatiable* hunger for knowledge. All of them, whether they have special academic talent or not, have this curiosity, this appetite for learning. They see that their parents have that same approach to their work, an avid passion for it. The children see that passion every day; they feel it. It's not something the parents go off and do elsewhere; it's right here. The children catch that passion and put it into what they do; it's the model they have to go by.

"The children here share their parents' intensity; they've absorbed it, and it's become part of their character. And I think this is very good! I don't think we have *enough* intensity in the world! We *need* people who are passionate and intense and *alive* and *jump* right into what they do. It's the best thing that could ever happen to children!"

Classical circus, with its dedications and masteries, stands gallantly, idiosyncratically opposed to any vision of life that divides creation — its races, ages, nationalities, and religions, its species — into compartments, in which they are inaccessible to one another. This is a frightened plan of the world. It is, to me, a frightening vision, as well; it wants to control and dehumanize us by drying us up — deanimalizing us, if you will — rationing and proscribing relationships, our ability to move freely and to learn, our knowledge of one another and of everything around us. This fearful view fuels the impulse to keep people and other animals separate from one another, enforcing a state of what Marthe Kiley-Worthington has aptly called animal apartheid. The clenched grip of fear ruins the capacity to delight in differences and difficult challenges; it hammers them into problems, sources of anxiety and suffering, which require convoluted, crazy solutions.

All of this, to me, is a nightmare. Massive structures rear up (what windows they have don't open, and if there are doors I can't find them), and everyone gets locked up inside, for our own "protection" and our own "good." In no time at all, we don't know what it is we're missing, though we're engulfed with the feeling of missing something. So we set to work, decorating the walls. We keep very, very busy doing this. When everyone calls the results Truth, or Love, or Justice, or Freedom — that's the worst part of the nightmare.

Who dares do combat with this? In the single ring of the classical circus, there is a gathering of artists whose job is to fight despair, to drive it away. It's a very different matter from, say, a mission to "create joy." The former concept involves a battle, on the scale of *The Faerie Queene*, with lucid, vivid power arrayed against what would defeat us.

Talking this over, one day, Paul Binder explained:

"We're brought together by two tenets: the first is economic survival — which is why all communities come together — and the second is the spiritual element — coming together to create something around a principle that's greater than our individual skills.

"Circus, more than any other art form, requires us to be a community. We build our lives around our nomadic existence. We need each other. And that's the way we work. That doubles when you work with animals, because if you work with them you must live with them, at all times. The regimen of travel and shows — teardown,

setup — requires that we're constantly mobile and we're constantly together. So that defines the necessities of our community. It takes organization beyond the comprehension of the greatest manager in the world. I say that because a manager can't create the environment, he can only support it. The individuals create the environment, and that's the culture of our organization when it succeeds. The success of The Big Apple Circus depends on the culture of the artists.

"We're building a company of artists who in a sense grow up with us, who share our goals and aspirations, and to the extent that they do, they're successful. People need to know the rationale behind the necessity for rules, for their own sakes and the survival of the company. When people don't understand the necessity for the survival of everyone involved, there are big disruptions, from the social environment all the way to the aesthetic environment. It's very difficult! So why do we persist in doing this? I think it's *necessary*. It reminds us of the roots of all important human interactions. Constantly! That's the circus's job!"

They carry on, then, because so much is at stake. Without the intensities of its forms and devotions, there would be no circus. Each artist, too, has to struggle with his or her own sense of despair. And then they have to manage to come together and go out and drive it away for the rest of us, over and over, night after night.

Binder paused, and then he said, "If, as a parent, you give in to an overwhelming sense of hopelessness, your children see that giving in is the currency. . . . Our job is not to give in."

No walls.

Just the ring.

Linda Hudes is the composer at The Big Apple Circus — "The Resident Genius," Paul calls her. The music is belted out by a lively group of virtuosi known as "Rick Albani and The Big Apple Circus All-Star Band." Everything that happens in the ring is heightened by the music emanating from the band, which sits on a platform above the *entrée des artistes* like a jazzy heavenly ensemble on a supervisory cloud. There are times of dreamy *pianissimo*, in the course of the show, a few moments of stunning and absolute silence, but mostly gay, expansive *fortissimo*. It's not something you listen to; you feel it inside and all around you. It accompanies your breathing and your pulse. When it starts up, after intermission, it tells you where you are. The music is the show's weather.

The next act, and the clown interlude following it, emphasize the variability in circus climate. Scheherazade's stories continue to be a travelogue of extremes. It begins

fortissimo with an act called The Dancing Gauchos, appearing in a parody of a Casablanca nightclub (with Mr. Stubs making a stab at being suave, à la Sidney Greenstreet, with a parrot on his shoulder), to amuse the sheik, who seems to have sunk into an advanced state of somnolent boredom. The idea is to wake him up, with the same kind of effect that thunderstorms and other explosions have on people.

The gauchos are loud, loud, *loud!* — even in contrast to what is not a quiet circus. Their costumes are of a shrieking, spangled red. Working in a tradition of Argentinian folk dance, the two men and one woman are equipped with — I should say armed with — huge drums, clattering high-heeled boots, and *bolas*, which they swing in beating rhythms, smacking them on the wooden floor. Spinning, lunging, stamping, rattling their *sabateo* heels, twirling their drumsticks, banging and booming, they produce a whole new level of racket. I stopped being a listener and became merely and completely a receiver of the beat, as if I too were a drum; I heard the drums pounding in my

stomach in much the same way you hear fireworks in there, not in your ears alone. This act, coming as it does right after the strolling relaxations of the intermission, shoots you back into the circus as if from a cannon. It's a shocking, manic way to shout, WELCOME BACK!!! and about halfway through you want to yell back, TOO MUCH NOISE IN HERE! but you know that would be no use. No one would hear you! Both wonderfully and close to intolerably, this pandemonium crashes on to a wildly danced rapid-fire overpowering climax. Then, blackout.

Silence. A low, dreamy arpeggio drifts into the air, rising, falling, rising again like a song from a glass harmonica. A single spot of moonlight illuminates Mr. Stubs and Gordoon, carefully stepping over the ring curb, off to one side over there. They are silently blowing bubbles, just— little — bubbles, with the kind of bubble-blowing rings you get at the dimestore. They dip their wands into their bottles, and bubbles begin to gather and mount in the air. They blow the bubbles gently upward to rise and drift slowly around. The single soft light catches them out of the dark and turns them all the colors of the rainbow. The clowns dance with the bubbles, alone with them, totally absorbed. In their goofy clothes, they move, now, not like

lords of misrule, but in tiny, formal measures, step by step, as if dancing a ritual. Their faces are peaceful benign masks of wonder. A single flute joins the harplike arpeggio and weaves itself in and out. The movements and music pay tribute to the bubbles: their delicacy, unpredictability, their prism tricks with light, their evanescence. It's a stately pantomime of the way you might walk among fireflies, or stars, perhaps unable to tell the difference.

Mr. Stubs and Gordoon blow bubbles back and forth to each other, gazing into each other's eyes. They take turns catching them, handling them as exquisite objects. Gordoon balances one on the end of his nose and smiles quietly, as if to himself, as it rests there. Then Mr. Stubs produces a bucket. He leans over, dips both hands in, then straightens, lifting his hands up before his face. Carefully, he blows. *Huge* bubbles appear, one at a time, shimmering globes that bob overhead. The audience says, not much louder than breathing, in a sort of low, atonal song, "Woowwww . . ." and, "Aaaahhhh. . . ."

Mr. Stubs lets a fat bubble alight on his hands, where it rests quivering in the light. Gordoon passes him another, and another. All the rocking globes become one, disappearing one into the other. More bubbles rise up, float along the music, the clowns following them across the ring with dignified steps. The mime concludes in front of the curtain, the two standing side by side, their right arms in unison rising over their heads in slow swings from one side to the other. Each pass produces bubbles quickly appearing one after another, like strung pearls, in shining, flyaway arcs. The clowns turn, then, in slow motion, look up, arms outstretched, toward what is disappearing. They are ravished, dazzled. Then, turning back toward us, they sink into deep, balletic bows. The soft music fills the whole airy ring. Then they're gone, except for a few drifting bubbles floating away.

Now. I do not mean to make a sermon about this. But these are — only — bubbles. And music, and dance, and light . . . It's just that people — are — sometimes — so — wonderful.

(And someday you should see what these guys do with a blow dryer and a roll of toilet paper.)

Suddenly, then, all the light turns silver, a trumpet fanfare soars above the arpeggios, and great billowing clouds of bubbles pour from nowhere — a swirling ceremonial to introduce Dolly Jacobs, "The Queen of the Air." She claims her realm by dropping veils and silver robe, standing before us in a shining bikini which is not so much a costume as an offhand decoration of something perfect. She takes hold of a white rope, hanging from above, and, holding her legs at a right angle to her body, one leg slightly bent, toes pointed, she climbs up, lifting herself hand over hand, to the Roman rings hanging far overhead.

During the first part of her act, the rings are stationary, and, hanging from them, by her hands or knees, she twists and swirls into lovely, impossible positions: backbends, splits, stag's leaps, flexible spirals. Perched on her rings, in between these sinuous windings of her body through the air, she pauses, gently swaying, and acknowledges, with open arms and gracious smile, the applause of the audience in a circle far below. She is a living example of the idea that an aristocrat never, never has to hurry. The rest of us down here on the ground may scurry about with our jaws clenched, clutching at our work, breathing fast, and complaining to our friends about how busy we are and about how there's not enough time to do what we want to do any more. That is not this woman's way. The space in midair forms around wherever it is she wants to be, and she makes time do her bidding.

From a vivid center below her lifted diaphragm, she breathes throughout her whole body, which is then a full extension, totally free from tension and hurry, of that breathing. Her movements require phenomenal strength (just try climbing a rope like that, for starters — without using your feet), and at some level we know that; but the effort is so deep down, so integrated and aware, that it appears as something new to us. It doesn't belong to one or another part of the body, but is diffused throughout it — throughout, that is, the entire personality. I have a young friend who managed to set aside stage fright and self-consciousness in order to play a Bach flute sonata at her grandfather's funeral, and she did it with dignity and skill. Someone said to me later, "I had no idea she was so tough." "Well, she's not tough," I replied, "she's well-trained, and she's strong." No amount of toughness would sustain the slow, long, measured breaths which Bach demands of a flautist; only deep, thorough power will do it. I'm reminded of an old horsemen's expression. When a horse is moving beautifully, strong but relaxed, balanced mentally as well as physically, they say, "He's going well within himself." Dolly Jacobs goes well within herself, if anyone ever has. As she pauses for our applause, she tells us she knows exactly who she is up there, what she's doing, where she belongs.

In the second part of the act, she swings on the rings from what seems like one side of the sky to the other, hanging from hands or knees, turning, somersaulting, slicing through the light. These powerful and lilting swings, and her body's flexible amplitude, form an image of sensuous limitlessness. What can the body *not* do? The music, here, is a melody which one might call upon, at a dark time, as an *aide de mémoire* for freedom. It's a shimmering waltz in big eight-bar phrases, summoning up wide open spaces, open skies over uncluttered hills or prairies, the first star rising. Dolly's swift flights — unmediated by any net — show that in the air she can go exactly where she wants to go.

At the end of her act, the ringmaster calls for silence. He tells us that she will attempt a full flyaway midair somersault off the rings, a complete release, to catch and hold onto a vertical rope off to one side. (Unusually rare and difficult feats are often introduced as "attempts," circus once again acknowledging, and revering, the vividness of unedited experience. The audience seems to understand this completely, and will applaud the gallant effort of a courageous but failed try with total enthusiasm. Whining doesn't belong here, and everyone seems to know it.) Mr. Paul calls for complete silence. "*Silence, please,*" he says, slowly. He subdues the last murmurings with a soft, "*Hushhh. . . .*" We know that this is not done for effect. It's a necessity, and so we are made Dolly's partners in real, important concentration. And we're afraid, too; so once again an aerialist must carry that weight, as well as her own.

The power of the momentum she seeks and reaches for with her whole body carries her faster and higher still. In her concentration she's geared into a shaft or column, like light, of concentration, to which every part of her responds. Thinking and doing are one. She spins, twists, grabs the rope, and, with a flourish, her whole body makes a grand gesture of joy.

Thus she commands her realm of air.

This woman moves with the transcendent grace and strength of a dancer, and as such she creates what one might call an illusion of elegant ease. Actually, she challenges our sense of what illusion *is*. I was especially moved by her softly relaxed, curved fingers. Every dancer knows how tension flows out from the torso, through the arms, and stops, betraying its presence, in stiff, awkward fingers. You can see this betrayal in the rigidly splayed fingers of some figure skaters and gymnasts when they fix their hands in what are only unpleasant imitations of dance carriage. Just so, the helplessness of a newborn baby, in the face of the threat of being let fall, expresses itself in held breath, rigid back, and clawlike hands. The depth of Jacobs's strength and relaxation flows from a supple and breathing center all the way out through her soft hands, even when she's hanging upside down in midair.

This is not an illusion of ease. It is a fact. There's no faking it. As such, it is another example of the inescapable immediacy of circus art. In ballet, the prince, the dying swan, may collapse in puddles backstage. But onstage they are protected by the proscenium arch, and the distance from the audience, from any suggestion of animal effort. At their best, they seem to proclaim, For us, ordinary physical laws are irrelevant. Circus artists aren't allowed the dancers' illusionary distances, and I don't know whether they'd enjoy the distance if they had it. They are in the business not of make-believe, but of representing, in real bodies, human and otherwise, fantasies, in all their exactitude. If flying is to become real — that is, if you are to fly and *to mean it*—you may not transcend natural laws; you must explore, obey, and use them. Then we find out, through the visible effort of art, what is truly possible.

Ben Shahn, writing in *The Shape of Content* about the work of Alexander Calder, speaks of an aesthetic which might just as well be that of classical circus:

While its shapes and forms are of an abstract genre, its meaning involves that return to nature, to first principles, which seems to be an indispensable condition of any great work of art or movement in art. Calder, once an engineer himself, but also son and grandson of sculptors, undoubtedly brought to engineering an eye for beauty, a sensitivity to aesthetic meanings, which would wholly escape the usual engineer. Thus, in stress and balance, in sequences of motion, in other basic and natural and probably common principles, he saw tremendous aesthetic potentialities, and put them to work.

The result for us who watch the continuously inter-dependent movements, the varieties of form balanced daringly and with delicate precision, is to experience the perfect union of nature and art. Here is sculpture that creates endless patterns in space-time rhythms. Of course, Calder's own great sense of play enters into all this, adding its own peculiar gaiety of forms.

Ernestine Stodelle, the eminent dance teacher and critic, has cited this passage to me by way of explaining the aesthetic underlying modern dance, and I don't think it's a coincidence that when I lured Ernestine to The Big Apple Circus, she was entranced by Dolly Jacobs, and helped me to think about her work. Ernestine knows all about breath, about gravity, about concentration in a shaft of light, about strength. The other afternoon, while we were talking these matters over, Ernestine leaned forward, at the table where we were drinking coffee, placed both of her elegant hands firmly on the cloth, and said, "You see —*mastery is transformation.* . . ." It is also no coincidence, but a lovely congruence, that Calder himself adored the circus, as you can see from the one he made, which lives at the Whitney Museum in New York City.

It makes sense, then, that Shahn's description of stress and balance, sequence of motion, and other basic natural principles, put to work for the sake of realizing their aesthetic potentialities, is a good description of what goes on at the highest levels of classical dressage, which is the training of horses. A return to nature, in this sense, is no misty, millennial vision. It is, as Shahn rightly says, a return to first principles.

If Calder's mobiles call us to "watch the continuously inter-dependent movements, the varieties of form balanced daringly and with delicate precision," so do highly skilled jugglers. Wang Beozhu, Zhung Yinghui, and Hu Mei are members of one of the most celebrated acrobatic troupes in the People's Republic of China, the Railway Acrobatic Troupe, which is sponsored by China's National Railway System. (Has anyone thought of adapting this sense of priorities to help solve the problems of mass transit in America? Why *not*?) They are acrobats and jugglers who work with objects called water meteors. Imagine transparent little bowls, filled with red water. Two bowls are tied at either end of a cord a couple of yards long. Picking up the cord in the middle — so there's a bowl of water at each end — the juggler deftly twirls the bowls into the air, his fingers working fast where they hold the cord so that the bowls are spinning rapidly round in circles through the air. From the resulting centrifugal force, not one drop of water spills. By the same principle, when you swing a bucket of water around, hard, with your whole arm, the water stays in the bucket instead of landing on your head. This is a gross example of the basic principle which the Chinese elevate and elaborate.

Human beings seem endlessly ingenious in manipulating and mastering natural phenomena. Imagine the juggler spinning two ropes, with bowls of water at each end,

one in each hand. Now he's doing this rapid-fire manipulation while his partner does a one-handed handstand on his head, her other hand twirling her own bowls of water on their string. Somersaults and flips follow the same dictate: whatever you do, keep the water meteors spinning aloft at the same time. The water meteors become more and more elaborate — not just two bowls, but six, eight, ten, like a Ferris wheel beyond top speed, illuminated with bright little lights — and the artists, while standing on their hands, juggle them *with their feet*.

The dance with the water meteors involves a transformation: the objects being manipulated take on a life of their own. The art of juggling imbues objects with their own life. You're not just watching someone spin things or throw and catch things; rather, someone displays the glory of those things, as they seem to leap and twirl and tumble on their own. The juggler seems quite amazed and delighted at having called them to life and at inspiring them to multiply and to perform more and more unlikely gyrations. They, in turn, seem to inspire the juggler to increasingly improbable feats of deftness. It's a lot like listening to an imaginative thinker play with ideas.

The faces of the three people who perform these bizarre feats are alight with constant and compact smiles, benign expressions reminiscent of the archaic smiles on the faces of early Greek sculpture. These are not the wide, dashing grins we're used to — the ones that say, Ta-DAH! Their bodies, too, for all their extraordinary flexibility, maintain a sense of reticence. Their dance is a series of poses, displayed and held, which focuses on, and by contrast exaggerates, the wildly swinging meteors. The acrobats move in discreet little running steps and leaps, lit with delicate gesture. Hu Mei is more clothed than any other woman we have seen so far, or will see. Her white costume is bejeweled, and she is elaborately, precisely coiffed and made up, but her trousers and blouse leave no skin exposed. The act combines flamboyance (the gaudy meteors, multicolored lights) with a highly stylized, chaste reserve. Following Dolly Jacobs, they play with gravity in a way wholly opposite to hers; they stay covered up and down to earth, and cause *objects* to shine and fly. Everything centers on the dexterous, endless manipulations, with constantly moving wrists and fingers, of the meteors, and on their flight.

The Chinese bring with them an atmosphere of authentic foreignness. Their recorded music travels with them, and it comes from another world. It sounds like a simple repetitive folk dance, as guileless as their smiles. It makes me look twice and wonder, Where am I? just as I do when an entirely new set of birdsong, or insect song, greets me in a foreign country. Indeed, the Chinese music has a high-pitched, merry, monotonous quality reminiscent of birds or insects in chorus. The Chinese acrobats provide a much more vivid sense of their country than any number of books or travelogue movies. This happens because we're so close to them, because their music surrounds us, and also because they're performing in very particular ways, and the style and dynamics of the artistic expression, as it always does in circus, distills essences.

A Westerner watching them is apt to feel a sense of distance that arouses new kinds of attention and fascination. Later this year, I will happen upon another group of Chinese circus artists when they come to perform in the new show at Lincoln Center. All morning, in the tent where other people are rehearsing in the ring, they sit in and stroll around among the empty seats. They chat with one another, put their feet up. They're relaxing, passing the time, shooting the breeze. Each Chinese artist, however, has in each of his or her hands three white wands, like yardsticks, held straight up, and on the end of each wand, balanced and spinning, is a saucer. So each person is twirling six saucers at once. Their hands and wrists deftly twist, their fingers dance incessantly. They keep this up, nonstop, for the two hours I'm there, all the while chatting, getting up, wandering about, sitting down again. Not one saucer falls. The continuous intricate casual activity (which they must have been practicing most of their lives) reminds me of a long day when, feeling very seasick myself, I watched a number of Scottish ladies seated all in a row on the Caithness ferry. As the boat heaved and pitched its way across the Pentland Firth, they sat and knitted incredibly complicated Fair Isle sweaters, using as many different colors of yarn as there are sheep, chatting away nonstop in Gaelic, never once stopping to count their stitches, and never once dropping a stitch.

The storyteller of circus takes us there and back again, over and over. This time, when the Chinese adventure ends, the full company of clowns takes over the ring. We've caught glimpses of Oaf and Mr. Fish before, in short appearances, but now they come into their own. The character of Oaf is more than a little demented. He's costumed in insane-Elizabethan style. Below a tunic, he wears a pair of hugely puffed-out pantaloons, of a rich brocade material, which gather in below his knees. Then come a pair of bare skinny legs, bent in a permanent *demi-plié*, and turned-out feet in turned-up slippers. On his bald head, above his narrow face, there's a peaked cap, its point curved over slightly to one side, so that his head looks like an odd little fruit or vegetable with a crooked stem on top. Oaf moves out in a manic scamper, as if on malfunctioning ball bearings. His voice is somewhat high in pitch, and he speaks in slow, overenunciated, unaccented syllables. The effect is to make him sound as we all do when we're only just beginning to read out loud, but since he isn't doing that, but speaking, he sounds sweetly deranged.

The voice of Mr. Fish, on the other hand, is deep, gravelly, like a jazz bassoon in the lower registers. His costume is a variation on the theme of bandit: shirt and vest; long, full gaucho pants gathered into big boots; a wide, flashy sash. He has a big handlebar mustache and bushy eyebrows. His exaggerated strides, all heels and elbows, are reminiscent of the weird power in Groucho Marx's low, scudding walk. All of this could be a little threatening, but he's so affable! The hat underscores this: it's not a beret, exactly, but a sort of big floppy snood, beginning low on his forehead and hanging down over his collar. Its piratical, but also ridiculous. His grin, the gaiety of his strutting bombast — and the hat — rob him of menace.

Mr. Stubs, flapping about in his hobo burnoose, and the bouncy Gordoon in his seaside stripes, join Oaf and Mr. Fish, so that these four charming eccentrics, with all their idiosyncrasies, are all together, in full possession of the ring, for their extended "Clown Entrée." This will be a full-blown set of variations on the old slapstick theme of whisking a tablecloth out from under the glasses and dishes on a table, leaving everything there still intact. They begin with a few glasses, and, cautioning children in the audience that this is not what their parents mean when they ask them to clear the table, they work their way up to a towering stack of glasses and wine bottles on trays. Moving and calling in close ensemble, they toss words and objects among themselves with quick precision. The preface, each time, is a chant: *"Nooooo friction!"* followed by a chorus, after each successful flourish of the table-cloth: *"Smoooooth!"*

Then they say, "We've balanced glasses, we've bal-

anced bottles; now we'll do the same thing with —*a child*. We need a volunteer to help us out! We need an *unbreakable* child!" A circular garden of hands springs up instantly, waving wildly. They choose a small boy who says his name is Ethan. They seat Ethan on a little stepladder, atop the table. They show him how to sit and how to hold on; Oaf advises, in his uninflected squeak, "Hold-on-like-your-life-depends-on-it-Ha-Ha-Ha-Ha-Ha!" They ask the audience to practice repeating the prefatory words (which become a kind of prayer, because that is, after all, a child up there) — "Nooooo friction!" They let him rehearse the repetition of the line with which he will finish the feat: "Smoooooth." "One, two, three, HIT IT!" they cry. The first time, Ethan bends his head and speaks a guarded "Smooth" into the microphone. They say, "Try it again." The second time, he seizes the microphone from Mr. Stubs, takes a big breath, and lets out a great big "*Smooooth*." We all give him a big round of applause.

I wonder about Ethan. Initially, I'm suspicious: would they dare try this with a randomly chosen child? He's a plant, surely? I thought this because I was unfamiliar with this old, old tradition of the one-ring circus. It soon becomes obvious that he's no plant; he's Ethan, reserved and tentative, at first, but soon rising to the occasion of being singled out and starred. He's just a kid who came to the circus and ended up in the middle of the ring. Which of us, as child or adult, has not imagined at least once, at a concert or play, what would happen if he sprang up from the audience and ran down the aisle and jumped onstage and joined the conductors or acts or dancers? There isn't an absolute barrier between circus audience and performers, because we're so engaged in helping to hold the whole thing together, as participants in ritual. Nonetheless, there is this dream of leaving your seat, springing into the light. With the help of the clowns, one of us, a child envoy, gets to act this out.

Because he isn't a trick, however, and is actually Ethan, he crosses over with small gestures of hesitation and anxiety, along with his pleasure. Watching this, we experience moments of concern ourselves, because our emissary is also the clowns' hostage. We want to trust them, to believe them to be Ethan's reliable custodians. They seem like nice people, and, after all, clowns are supposed to be friends to children. And it's good to see that these guys are totally unlike those loud, bloated clowns who laugh and laugh and make children get smaller and smaller and smaller. The four engage the child wittily, personably. But—they are clowns, after all, manic people beyond the fringe, who think it's fun to be on the verge of whipping a cloth out from underneath a child sitting way up on a stepladder on top of a table. They might be, all five of them in there, children, and maybe someone ought to stop them, before they hurt themselves. (Sure enough, the ringmaster comes in and stands in the background, arms folded across his chest; you know he's there to keep an eye on things.) We're still wondering, though, Are they going to know not to do something crazy with Ethan?

It's a very funny scene indeed, but the enthusiasm with which the audience joins in the chants (*"Nooooo friction!"* *"Smoooooth!"*) isn't passive, the way laughing at something might be. It's active and protective, because that's our child, that's us, up there.

Now the clowns bestow on Ethan a round red false nose and Mr. Stubs's floppy hat, clothing him so that he becomes a clown, too, while remaining, incongruously, Ethan. The audience roars, *"Nooooo friction!"* Drums roll. Ethan grips the seat, hunches, ready. They jerk the tablecloth out from underneath him with a flourish, leaving him safe and enthroned. "One, two, three, HIT IT!" they cry. With a huge grin, he seizes the microphone, takes in a terrific breath, and sings out, "SMOOOOOTH!" as loud as he can, for as long as he can. Trumpets blare. The rest of us go bananas, cheering. Up go the ringmaster's arms, in celebration.

And the clowns do one last, lovely thing. Steering him gently into place, they show Ethan how to make a traditional courtly bow to the audience, one arm in front of his waist, one arm in back. You have learned to perform in the ring for this instant, they seem to say, so you must also learn the formalities, the etiquette of it. Then this goon quartet frames his bow (as he repeats it with panache) with their own broad gestures of appreciation for his good work.

You may wonder, as I did, how the clowns decide whom to pick out from the audience. Aside from the dictates of size, they have no formula at all. They have learned to guard against a phenomenon which shocked me when John Lepiarz, who plays Mr. Fish, told me about it. "I won't choose a child who doesn't want to be chosen. I'm very aware of parents who put kids' hands up for them. Then it's not for the kids, it's for the parents. No, never them." The clowns learn to read faces quickly and to judge whether a child will work out. "You're there to entertain, not to humiliate, and an unwilling volunteer is nothing more than a victim. That's not what we do."

Have they ever picked the wrong person? A child for whom the whole scene is just too much? It has happened, once or twice, but then they quickly, tactfully choose another, and they are exquisitely sensitive to the pressures the child is up against. David Casey, Oaf's creator, said, "It's not that kids perceive the tablecloth thing as dangerous. When the clowns ask for volunteers and all the kids put their hands up, each kid is part of that. But then if suddenly you're selected, it's a shock! You didn't expect to win the lottery! The lights are overwhelming, you're surrounded by this huge ocean of faces, and these strangers are telling you what to do."

I remember one little girl who responded to being in the ring with distinctive bravura, showing great promise for her future career as a grown woman. Right before the tablecloth was pulled away, she leaned over, shook a small finger at Mr. Stubs, and commanded, loudly, *"Don't you drop me, now!"* Ethan is not so outgoing. His grin, when it finally appears on his somber face, is simply wonderful to behold. I wonder, as he scrambles back to his seat, what kind of memory this night has left to blossom in that small head.

It won't ruin everything for you, will it, if I point out, here, that Mr. Stubs, Gordoon, Mr. Fish, and Oaf are all highly trained professionals? that they really do know what they're doing? Will it spoil anything to hear David Casey say, "People always tell me, 'Gee, it looks like you're having a good time out there,' and I reply, 'Of *course* it looks like I'm having a good time! I'm an *actor*!'" In several other shows of The Big Apple Circus, there was a delectable clown named Grandma, played by a witty, tense, hardworking person named Barry Lubin, an actor of great canniness and skill. He said to me one evening (still in his curly gray wig and red *shmatte*), "You have to be *so* sensitive to the audience, *so* exact in your timing. If you play it for sad or for funny, you're dead on your feet! Same as when an animal trainer or an animal isn't paying attention, he really is *dead*. I mean, you put your life on the line, out there!"

What is it about clowns that makes this so hard to believe? Once I saw Oaf and Mr. Fish accidentally splatter a man in the audience with a broken egg, and I was surprised to find them lamenting this, backstage, so easy was it for me to assume that they're the sort of people who take particular joy in making messes. "Of course not!" Lepiarz said crossly, "We're here to make people happy, and it's *disgusting* to get egg thrown at you!" In the presence of good clowning, artistic intention slips out of sight behind their winning ways. Interestingly, we're apt to think of animals in much the same way, imagining that they, like clowns, can't help what they do, that they don't know any better.

In animal movies, we have The Brilliant Sensitive Dog (as in the endearing "Lassie" series) or, more recently, in a contemporary reversal of the ideal, The Large Sloppy Out-of-Control Dog (such as "Beethoven.") In either case, these characters are made up of highly trained dogs working, along with their trainers, to create an illusion — the illusion being that since they're dogs, everything about them is spontaneous, and they are who they are. If it's hard to imagine that what you're watching may not be real, in that sense, it's because they're so good at their work. Good clowns are master craftsmen, artists in command of carefully refined techniques, skills, and traditions, of a very particular kind.

The old story about the clown laughing on the outside while crying on the inside may be just as false, or irrelevant, as the idea of a clown being constantly happy. Nei-

ther vision takes his professionalism, and his person-
hood, which is out of our reach, into account, just as the
images of Lassie-as-perfect and Lassie-as-abused are
both wide of the mark of Lassie-the-dog, who was a sometimes difficult, but well-trained and hardworking male
collie named Lad. Most of us don't have any trouble
knowing Olivier from Hamlet; we can even sort out Sean
Connery from James Bond if we think it over. But bring
in animals and clowns, and there's a great confusion, because of the notion that they're all just doing what comes
naturally.

A few years ago, various of my friends urged me to go
to the Yale Repertory theater to see a production of Molière's *Scapin*, because they said it was done like a traditional circus and I would love it. On the stage was a faint,
painted suggestion of a circus ring, and small groups of
theatergoers were seated onstage nearby. The clown
characters pulled people out of these seats and used them
in the play as foils to bounce jokes off of.

Everyone I had talked to seemed to love this, so I was
surprised to see how cranky it made me. I sat outside at intermission and brooded about why this production was
being praised to the skies, in reviews and here in acade-

mia, when it didn't seem to me to get the circus idea right. It looked to me like a bit of ornamentation randomly pinned onto Molière's play, and (my tantrum continued) people don't recognize it because they don't know where all of this comes from or how it ought to be. The actors are doing their best, but when they bring people onstage, they're not making room for them; they're steamrolling right over them; and so nothing develops, nothing is revealed. The game of using the audience is an old, complex tradition of clowning, and no matter how ridiculous it gets, the stranger introduced to the ring is never an object. Because the tradition isn't there, the Molière doesn't work. It's like a failure of horse training, in many ways. Perhaps (I concluded, crossly) the trouble all comes from a fatal error right at the start: that ring in there — that charming, decorative bit of business — that ring, you know — you ought to know — is supposed to be for horses. . . .

Now — the elephants.

As I write this, it has become four in the morning; a predawn rain with a cold breeze has come up outside the screened porch where I'm sitting. So I go to find some-thing to put around my shoulders, and fetch up with my barn coat, which, I notice happily, the smell of horses thoroughly pervades. You might ask, "What is it, about horses?" and I might reply, "Here, put this coat on." But how will you react to that? I mention this for the sake of some sort of truth in advertising, in order to acknowledge that there are large segments of the population to whom my coat (as opposed to the idea of horses) might not be the comfort that it is to me, and to whom the threat of a life without the real presence of animals might not be a cause for grieving. That these segments may, in fact, be enlarg-ing is my cause for grieving.

Clive Barnes, in a thoughtful article in the *New York Post* about the crucial presence of animals in circus, wrote, "We have seen animals at home, animals at work, animals on exhibition, but there were animals collaborating with men, on at least an equal basis." The Big Apple Circus has always featured animals (and, as I've said, this is true of circus by definition); but the fact of their working on at least an equal basis with people is a telling point, and par-ticularly vivid with respect to this show. One way to ex-plain it is to say that the oddity of atmosphere, here, allows the performers to take the risk (and to take us with them) of exploring what it means for all of us to be creatures. Another way is to say that just as the human performers are extremely, often bizarrely, real —*super*natural, literally and figuratively—so are the animals, but more so. Circus acknowledges this by featuring them as "at least" our equals; by implication, in some areas of expression, they completely surpass us. We creatures are not all the same. What stretches the audience's imagination — and the show pulls and lures and seduces the imagination to do this—is to know all the ways in which its creatures, all of them, are valuable and real.

After watching—a generic and insufficient word for the complexity of what one does—Toto and Peggy, the two elephants, and Bill Woodcock, their trainer, work together, I know a great deal more about elephants than I ever did before, which is to say, I have become fascinated by elephants.

Peggy and Toto, like Anna May, are Asian elephants. Their heads are domed and broad of face, alongside which their ears have a certain scallopy delicacy. Their eyes are small, curiously placed miles apart, on either side of their great philosophical foreheads. They have long, elegant eyelashes, and an expression which is at once intent, shrewd, and introspective. Their trunks are not incongruous, not added on, but a fluid, muscular extension of this expression, swinging and lifting in powerful movements that reveal the surprisingly supple energy of their whole bodies. Trunks seem to have a whole repertoire of nuanced gestures of which a novice observer can catch only glimpses. It's as if the trunk combines in one entity the manipulative and the communicative power of our hands and our mouths, with exaggerated potential, of a distinctively elephantine kind, for everything from reticent to flamboyant meanings.

The skins of elephants are crumpled, draped, and complicated, like a mountainous landscape observed from miles up in the air. Wonderfully, they are also covered with hair. They are not simply gray, but have distinctive mottlings and frecklings. The great spines crest high as ridgetops, and their bottoms, with their tufty tails, are comfortably broad and substantial. Their feet are huge, flat, and bulbous, but are amazingly adept at feeling out, and balancing on, objects such as tiny stools. The articulation of their legs is fascinating, because it is so well oiled, and also because their hind legs bend at the knee about the same way a person's does, so the legs look a lot like a person's, in heavy gray trousers.

Elephants, as I have said before, smell absolutely wonderful. This is something that you are not apt to discover the details of from a book, a picture, a statue, or even the most artfully made movie. In the presence of animals, the shortcomings of human artistic forms are underlined by our inability to convey a vivid notion of the odors of things. There is, for example, no equivalent of onomatopoeia to encompass smell. This isn't surprising, I suppose, since alongside most animals our sense of smell is totally incompetent. We are so ignorant in this vast area of sense that we haven't even bothered to invent a word, a nasal equivalent of "deaf" or "blind," to name our impairment. My mother-in-law, Louise Field Cooper, used the word *snoof* to convey some of this meaning, as in, "he has such a bad cold he's gone totally snoof." But this does not encompass the sense of a permanent, inevitable, specieswide condition. In any case, the circus at least gives you the chance to use what little nose you have.

Elephants have a distinctly delicate, deft tread. Theirs is a way of going that nicely combines insouciant ambling with a relentless, deliberate *forwardness*. I have mentioned how hard it seems for people to understand and respect the fact that elephants are very, very big. It helps to see them moving, close up, because the magnitude of their progress dwarfs their path. This is not just movement; it's travel. I am reminded of Isak Dinesen's description of elephants in Africa "pacing along as if they had an appointment at the end of the world."

I should also say that Peggy and Toto in the ring, along with Anna May, earlier, make it quite clear that all elephants are not the same, any more than all people are. These are individuals. As you begin to notice subtle differences among them in size, color, shape, and style, you become aware, just as you do with people, that there is a myriad of things you do not know about them, that you cannot and will not know.

So elephants, close up, are wonderful in themselves. But something is happening, here, to fuel and complicate wonder: we witness animals and people working together. Peggy and Toto dance, in a sort of interspecies *pas de quatre*, with two small and vivid acrobats named Marie-Pierre Benac and David Dimitri. Bill Woodcock is the act's conductor. He moves about the ring in slow accord with the elephants, with an eye both to them and to the acrobats tumbling on and around them. He's acting as both trainer and interpreter, attending to the different understandings in the ring with him. His expression, both serious and abstracted, is characteristic of all animal trainers when they're deep in their work, focused on the animals and their human partners and what they are all creating together.

The elephants convey a similar concentration, on a grander scale. Toto and Peggy amble slowly along, side by side, swinging and turning, as David, a dashing fellow, standing with one foot on each elephant, absorbs the swaying motion of the two great backs in the strength of his widespread, supple legs and pelvis. He, in turn, provides a base for Marie-Pierre, whom he lifts and balances on his shoulders and hands. Her petite body is all grace and readiness. Her movements and gestures, at the pinnacle of the elephant-human pyramid, lightly reflect and respond to each motion, from its origin on the ground, its complicated travel through Peggy and Toto, and then through David. Hers is an elegant, careful improvisation danced to the slow rhythms of the elephants as they come to her through the body of David.

It seems profoundly suitable that Marie-Pierre and

David should be dressed as Southeast Asian wedding dancers and use the formal gestures — flexed feet with toes upturned, lifted arms, turned heads, hyperextended fingers — of traditional temple dance. This style reveals the ceremonial nature of the process by which members of different species may dance together, and it pays tribute, by reference, to the ancient association of Asian elephants and people, in work and ceremony, in those countries where they live together. At one point, Marie-Pierre holds a kneeling arabesque within the curve of Peggy's uplifted trunk; she faces David, who salutes her in the same attitude from his location behind Peggy's ears. The long horizontal plane of the elephant's lifted head and the careful curve of her trunk support the dancers in their mirrored poses, and they are lit by the intelligent upward glance of her eye.

I notice a special gesture which an elephant uses to help a person leap aboard her back. Peggy graciously proffers one large foot for Marie-Pierre to hop up on. Then an elegant little flip of the great gray wrist propels the woman upward. This small, stylish variation on giving, and getting, a "leg up" (by which you might put out your hands in a cradle, for me to put my knee into, so that you could toss me up onto a horse's back) symbolizes the vital sense of connection between species which is the soul of the act. Because of the elephant's grandeur, the delicacy with which she holds her huge foot out to the tiny person is infinitely expressive of *politesse*. So a giant, his nobility transcending any hint of condescension, on one hand, or subjection, on the other, might offer to help a midget. There is something delightfully offhand and companionable about it. Peggy says to Marie-Pierre, Up you go! The gesture seems to say, We have worked this out together. Commanded and commanding, we two species are on mutual ground.

The *pas de quatre* conveys a fantasy of people and elephants being together. But truth is fantasy's wellspring. The act arises from, and encompasses, real possibilities for the fluid interplay of animal and human intention. The dance is believable because it so obviously has its origins in substantial, not factitious, relationships. When Toto performs a handstand on a pedestal, and David, at the same moment of the elephant's upside-down lift, rises upside down to his own handstand on Toto's head, they stay

exactly together, to show each species' version of the odd art of balancing upside down. The synchrony of their work together is no illusion, but the truth.

In order to understand the climax of this act, for which everything is now being arranged, it will help if you will try to call to mind an old acrobatic trick. You've probably seen it before. There's a seesaw, more properly called a teeterboard. At one end the board is on the ground, because a person is standing on it, facing the other end, which is up in the air. Someone runs out and does a pouncing leap, which punches the upper end of the teeterboard down. That force, which the acrobat meets with his own energy upward, propels him up into the air. He does a backward somersault in midair and lands on the shoulders of a third man who's been standing in knee-bent, arm-lifted readiness to catch him.

A splendid variation of this trick happens now. David is the man on the seesaw; Peggy, standing firm right behind him, will be his landing place. Most wonderfully, it is Toto who will run forward, from way back behind the open curtain, to plant a great foot on the end of the teeterboard, sending David into the air.

This sequence requires subtle cooperations among

everyone involved: acrobat, elephants, and trainer. In order for it to succeed, everyone depends on everyone else. Peggy, the catcher, must know what's coming, be ready for it, and stay firmly and absolutely still. Also, if David were relying on another man to push the teeterboard down, the two of them would have conventional calls and signals at their disposal. The acrobat has to be able to know exactly what's coming, and when, to be able to react to it; he can't behave like a passively tossed object, because he'd be injured if he did. But in this case, the acrobat must be in sensitive communication not only with Bill — another person — but also with another key participant, Toto — an elephant — who will send him where he wants to go.

In the long moment of preparation, while the drums roll and the audience falls silent, Toto shifts his weight slightly from side to side, like a tennis player awaiting a big serve. His head and trunk are lifted high and at a slightly oblique angle, in an attitude of intense concentration, which accommodates both the target ahead of him and Woodcock, standing right beside him, poised to run. Peggy, Toto, David, and Bill are suspended in a sort of salute, a focused readiness-to-go. Now Bill gives the go-ahead. Toto runs into the ring, head held high, and, with tremendous athletic precision, he rears up in a fluid motion of acceleration and stamps one great foot on the end of the teeterboard. David, ready for him, crouches and springs with equal exactitude, and up he goes — spinning — to land lightly on the high ridged hill who is Peggy.

As the audience breaks loose in a cheering, whistling salute to this tour de force, some of us may consider all the things that could have gone wrong, but did not, and why. Timing is everything, timing and absolute accuracy. Peggy must know her job; she must be resolute in her stance, absolutely steady, come what may, or all would be lost. Toto has to know how to hit the teeterboard — at what moment, where, with what amount of force — or David would end up either in the bleachers behind Peggy or off to one side or flat on the ground. Just as he is not a passive object, a catapulted sack of potatoes, so Toto is no machine to be driven forward trucklike with Woodcock's foot on the accelerator. Toto has to be a live, sentient participant, or nothing will work. And Bill (who, through knowing Toto, has taught him what he needs to know) has to be an exact interpreter between elephant and man, in order to help Toto to arrive at just the right place at the right time with just the right amount of force.

This artistic feat, performed by highly trained — that is, educated — people and animals together, is an illumination of the knowingness permeating vastly different bodies and minds. It floods us with sudden knowledge about the glory inherent in our being — people and animals — in the world together.

Like the camel and horse acts that came before, this elephant act shows that classical circus is *about* our relationship with animals. It is the art form whose very subject is this relationship. Circus wouldn't exist without these animals, and it also expresses and reveals them, in all their mystery and beauty. And so the question I am often asked — Does circus offend the dignity of animals? — seems to me to miss the point. The dignity of animals, as circus reveals, is innate, glorious, and indestructible. And at one and the same time, dignity is irrelevant to them.

For example, in order for you to experience the glory of horses more fully, I would like for you to see an *haute école* act, the dance of the most highly schooled horse and rider, which has come, with circus directly on its route, from a long tradition of horsemanship as a performing art, predating by centuries the contemporary scene of competitive dressage. It is the classical *haute école* that the white Lipizzaner stallions perform, at the Spanish Riding School in Vienna. The fact is, however, that at the time of The Thousand and One Nights, Katja Schumann does not yet have a horse at the requisite level of training, so you see no solo horse act, tonight. Khan, the chestnut stallion who will one day become Katja's high school horse, is still a youngster, part of the Liberty act. In time, his training will reveal his special capacities, and he will go on to become a spirited and versatile performer of the *haute école*. Right now, though, he's still in the *corps de ballet*, where he belongs. There are no shortcuts in the correct training of horses. It would be an offense to this fine horse to put him prematurely into work for which he is not yet physically or mentally ready; or to have him work the wrong way, that is, not up to the high standard of tradition; or to fail to recognize his talent and not to have him do the work at all. This sensitive, strong-minded stallion will, one day, be totally committed to his work, and will give his work everything he's got, and it will be beautiful.

Thus will he be honored as he deserves. But his dignity is not something that concerns him. While I have known many proud horses, and certain vain ones, and while all horses are tremendously sensitive animals, I have never known one to stand on his dignity the way people do — that is, defensively. I suspect that dignity is not an issue for other animals, the way it is for people. Perhaps they trust God more than we do. Perhaps to worry about dignity is to misunderstand and suspect the intentions of the divine, and the nature of the world, in a way that animals know better than to do. Walt Whitman said of animals, in *Leaves of Grass*,

They do not sweat and whine about their condition,
They do not lie awake in the dark and weep for their sins,
They do not make me sick discussing their duty to God. . . .
Not one is respectable or unhappy over the whole earth.

Animals are the absurd and the divine, in one. They are the grotesque and the ethereally beautiful, in a single, self-contained form. Anyone who has a dog has seen it: one minute the dog is splendidly alert and noble, hearing something beyond our ken out in the night, and the next minute he's scratching at a flea, licking his bottom. At the circus, the absurd and the divine live together all the time. There is Toto balancing on his hind legs, isolated by the spotlight, the better to show his full magnificence. Elephants seem to know all about this wholeness; they represent and embody it. It's no accident that Karen Blixen, after years spent living with the land, animals, and people of an inescapably natural world, in Africa, chose for herself the pen name Isak, which means "God laughs." God laughs. We don't always get the jokes, and we often blame this on God. Animals are, perhaps, more reverent, on this score, than most of us find it possible to be.

We make animals into icons — of nobility, cuddliness, freedom, whatever is bothering us at the moment — in a way that says much more about what we care about, worry about, or worship, or fear, or desire, than about anything that matters to animals themselves. All our worst fantasies (frightened, frightening, sadistic, imprisoned, angry) and our best ones, too (freedom, nature, peace) — all fueled by guilt and despair at the state of the world, and an amorphous feeling of things being out of control — consolidate into ideologies, which focus on animals, and run amok there.

One day, a cross-looking woman peered through the

chain-link fence at Van Cortland Park, in the Bronx, at the circus horses eating their afternoon hay, in their shady stalls under the horse tent. It was a hot, dirty day, full of traffic and noise outside the park, but cool and airy where the horses were peacefully munching away in their orderly world. This woman called me over to the fence and muttered fiercely, "Those horses should *not* be locked up in there. Somebody ought to let them loose so they could run *free*." In the Bronx? I thought, and looked around to see where the guard was. And wondered whether she hated her job, or her apartment, or her family, or her life, so ready was she to assume without knowing them that these horses hated theirs.

I should like to tell another story now, to add to Scheherazade's array, before this show is over. It involves going to a park in Geneva, Switzerland, where the wonderful Circus Knie was playing, featuring as always many different sorts of animals, who live on the lot in a traveling zoo which is open for the public to visit.

Late one afternoon, when the crowds had thinned out, during the quiet time before the evening show began, I spent some time watching the lions. The first thing I noticed was that the lions hadn't the least interest in watching *me*. Something about their profound, contemplative gaze, well over and beyond me, put me on my best behavior. I was aware of wishing to measure up. Several little boys wandered by, who didn't like being thus ignored. They whistled, chirped, clapped their hands. Then they, too, in the presence of the large, reserved feline faces, settled and took to gazing (but you could tell it took an effort on their part). I wondered, What is it about my species, that we want so badly to have animals notice us? We with the words and the hands — what is it about us?

The lions continued to muse. Some were fast asleep, over on their backs, their great blond bellies turned upward, their broad paws flopped in total relaxation. Others sat gazing, blinking occasionally. I stood and wondered about that look, which seems to go for miles, and about the roar designed for wide, open spaces; and, of course, I wondered about the cages. You can't look for very long at lions without imagining open skies and plains — something that ought to be there, but isn't. The bars look like a hideous mistake.

Now, these particular lions are from the Clubb-

Chipperfield organization, in England, which supplies trained animal acts to circuses. The lions are English born and bred and have never been anywhere near Africa. (In a visit several years later to the house of Mary Chipperfield, the great trainer of wild cats, I noticed deep stratified gouges in the legs of a big desk in the study. Her husband, Roger Cawley, shook his head, smiling ruefully. "Lion cubs," he murmured; "*so* destructive." But when I was in Geneva, I didn't know any of that, yet.)

So you're apt to think, watching them in Geneva: Africa is where they belong. How would that be arranged? It's so difficult to control guilt that it runs all over, making up dreams on the lions' behalf. Wiltshire doesn't cross my mind; I imagine they dream of a veldt.

But then I remind myself: In the here and now, whose dream is this, anyway? I look, try really to attend to, those reserved, implacable faces. How can I presume to know the contents of their dreaming? What makes me think I know—when I know nothing about lions—and when I don't know these lions?

So I talk with the people who do, and I learn something very interesting. Space, they say, is not what matters most to a lion. It's nice, but the most crucial thing is security. A place that's his or hers, into which no one else can intrude. This is true in the wild, which is not an unmarked, measureless place without limits, but something that lions divide, claim, defend, and fight over, as they do, also, about each other.

The ring is the trainer's place, and the lions respect that. Their cages are theirs, and he respects that. Even square footage (which is regulated by law, in Switzerland) is not the first thing that counts for them; inviolate ownership does. A lion trainer would say that if he were to put a hand in one of those cages without first asking the lion's permission, and the lion bit off his hand, justice would recognize that the lion was acting within his rights and was welcome to it.

Now, this bit of lion information, arising from long acquaintance and experience, is not something I can imagine. I can learn it, but I can't dream it up staring at lions. I can dream only my own dreams, which are largely concerned with a different vision of freedom and a different definition of rights. Come to think of it, it does seem to make sense. I, for instance, might prefer a large house to a small apartment, and other things might be desirable, too — in my case, big windows, white walls, wood floors, and perhaps a garden. But the really basic, most important requirement is that *no one come into the place where I live without being invited*.

This makes real and practical sense, but it doesn't automatically occur to me that a wild animal might be concerned — even more than I, perhaps — with such practicalities. Whereas any creature with survival on her mind *has* to think in these terms. Nor can she just come and go as she pleases. Lions have to consider where the next drink and the next meal are coming from, the welfare of their children, what the neighbors are like. Indeed, Elizabeth Marshall Thomas, in a fascinating essay about the lions and Bushmen of the Kalahari desert, argues that until both groups were disrupted in recent decades, the lions and people of that area had for centuries worked out complicated forms of correct behavior on both sides, which can be considered cultural in both cases. A set of complex mutual restraints made it possible for them to occupy common ground. The lion's place was never postmillennial, much as we might wish it.

As an American, perhaps, I'm particularly preoccupied with the idea of freedom as the notion of being allowed to go anywhere I want to go, to live wherever I like and as I please, untrammeled by anyone else, and with a romantic notion of limitless space. In fact, I even think I have the right to life, liberty, and the pursuit of happiness, and I'm devoted to the idea of having a whole vast continent behind me to prove it. So the lion — with the image of his attendant veldt invisibly hovering behind his reserved gaze — gives me the feeling that he shares this preoccupation, but in an even bigger, more tragic way. I think I can interpret his dreams without asking him for details — without asking him, as it were, for his own associations over a long period of time in which I might learn something of how his mind works, and how his is different from mine.

So let's say that I really feel terribly sorry for this poor lion in his cage — and I reach in to liberate him, and he lashes out at me. I think (contemplating the place where my hand used to be), "Poor lion; he's angry; he's imprisoned; he wants to be back on the veldt; what right have I to keep him here?" I hope I would know that I made a mistake to mess with him, but I still might not know what the mistake was. I might not know — because I don't know lions — that my error was in violating his free territory — the place that belongs to him — the security of which must never be impinged upon — that is, his cage.

So why can't we arrange it so that lions have to talk only with other lions, French-speaking people with other French-speaking people? Because the world won't allow it. Because it's a small world; we're all nomads in it, and strangers, and we have to learn to communicate when the need arises, or perish of loneliness or other forms of desolation and destruction.

When we train animals, we say, Okay, no matter how you've ended up here with me, or why, it's your world, too; it looks like we're in it together; so we'd better engage in learning to understand each other. We need to learn each other's rules and manners, when to mind our own business, how to do each other no harm, how to help each other out. Perhaps dogs are especially well equipped to deal with these matters-of-fact because they're like the Swiss — forced by their historical locations into developing a knack for being multilingual.

People who work with animals tend to be down-to-earth, to a degree directly proportionate to what they and their animals have at stake together. Trainers who do the best work believe there's something real to know about animals, something worth carefully attending to; that some things are true, others not, which they know on the basis of education, close observation, and daily experience; that it's important — a matter of life and death, in some cases — to know the difference between truth and hallucination and to act accordingly at all times. Though deeply acquainted with the mysterious, they are suspicious of obfuscation, and they don't quibble about the existence of reality. They are Natural Philosophers, convinced of the existence of Natural Law. Their lives, and those of the animals in their care, depend on the depth of these convictions. So, arguably, animal trainers are not modern people; their culture is not modern, either. The impulse to abolish the understandings, wisdoms, and ways of traditional cultures may be part of the energy being devoted, now, to getting rid of such people and what they believe in and what they do.

One morning a few years ago, I was rubbing the mud off of Badger, a Welsh Cardigan Corgi, after a long ramble around the farm, and I thought about how dogs and horses carry an aura around them of the landscape where they seem to belong. Badger expressed himself most vividly as a dog of the Welsh countryside in its most rural precincts. He was a cattle-herding dog, who seemed to need not only that activity but that landscape around him in order to be most himself. The house and all its habits filled him with angst. The barn, though, and navigating a rough pasture in a sleet storm, running circles around the heifers to bunch them up — all that filled him with joy. Roughness, a good fight, gave him pleasure; sweetness made him growl in dismay. He would have been quite content to live in a stone hut, to go out in all weathers with a crusty old cowman. I knew all that, faced facts, and trained him accordingly. I gave him the disciplines and duties he craved, and thus gave him a place in the world. I couldn't give him a Welsh hillside; that's just the way things were. He continued, however, to inform me about that place, or he seemed to. He was a grand dog, but haunted.

As the landscapes disappear, the animals who had jobs there are the refugees. I'm not talking about what's the "natural" way for them to live, but about the circle — of animals, people, work, and the right landscape — that is, the culture — from which one or another part is removed, leaving holes. I mean the *pentimento* of a landscape surrounding the animals who end up with us, wherever we are, in another place, and without the old devotions.

There is a certain spooky feeling about circus and the animal work in it. Perhaps this is because it is an art form

which says, right out, that the old landscapes no longer exist, or do not exist in the way we would like to imagine them. The lioness, whose job on the Serengeti Plain is to hunt and to pass on her genotype, will have another job among us, carrying her haunting imagery with her, as Badger brought a windswept Welsh hillside to me. Circus speaks the truth about these matters, and it's almost unbearable.

Circus is classical, in this way, not romantic, not modern in the least. Not that it's artificial and unnatural — those are completely romantic constructs. Circus predates such notions. It says, This is what is. It originated at a time when all sort of old forms were being turned upside down. Drawing on these forms, it put them in a ring right before people to entertain them with what they were about to lose. And it had its golden age at the end of the nineteenth century, inspiring longing and desire in people who understood that the world they knew really was on the way out. Now, in the late twentieth century, it makes some people simply too uneasy, because they cannot tolerate the pain of what is lost. Tragedy is unfashionable, in a sentimental time.

I have seen, for example, dog owners physically recoil — I mean, reel back as if they'd been slapped — at being told that love may not be as important to their dogs as respect. The idea that love is *not* all you need — that an animal might place higher value on a mutually dependent and respectful working relationship — is, to some people, completely offensive. I may love my animals, but what I have with them, the shape of that love, is private, just as it is with my husband or my children. It's between us, and not a subject for parade, or a way to prove a point. Donald McCaig, in *Eminent Dogs, Dangerous Men*, talks about Jimmy Wilson "and his grand bitch, Peg," a shepherd

and his sheepdog. "Nobody has ever seen him give Peg a
pat," McCaig says, and then "the mild man looked up
with a quiet smile. 'Why, do you think Peg doesn't know
what I think of her?'" This is not, sadly, a modern way of
thinking.

I once heard the poet Alan Dugan say that we live in a
violent and sentimental society. He was talking about a
place where someone can say, "I love you, I love you,
baby, I love you"—and then beat you up.

As an antidote to such a statement, I offer something
Katja Schumann said which it seems right to arrange in a
particular form:

> *Of course we love the horses,*
> *but they are not pets;*
> *they are colleagues.*
>
> *They need me in order to eat,*
> *And I need them in order to eat.*
>
> *They are colleagues*
> *with their own needs and ways*
> *and their own ways of living*
>
> *and part of that life*
> *we do together.*

These words, lucid and quiet, come from the world of the ring. Circus demonstrates that there are ways for people and animals living with one another to behave, to prosper, to create something valuable together. It invents a landscape within which species operate — not by murder and mayhem, nor by isolation, nor by sentimentality — but with this firm resolve: *we will stay here together*. This is courage in the face of the constant possibility of tragedy. It is a world in which animals and people have, together, a stake

in something real, and in which something real is always at stake.

The landscape is constantly being reinvented. Wherever they put the ring, there it is.

I should say here, and it is by no means an afterthought, that yes, cruelty to animals is possible. Cruelty exists in the world, as do bad art and other corruptions. Any good circus trainer, however, knows one very important thing about cruelty: it doesn't work. It produces only bad results, and cannot produce good ones. A trainer not in control of his or her own impulses gives rise to ugliness, among other offenses and disasters. However, the assumption that *any* work with animals, *any* appearance of them in performance, *any* training, is by definition cruel, is not only untrue; it is dangerous. And it has become wantonly common.

One morning, a class of schoolchildren was visiting the lot at The Circus Knie, and one small boy — around seven or eight years old, I guess — was found to be sobbing as he stood next to the large grassy enclosure, where the elephants were going to work on one of the biweekly truckloads of freshly cut saplings that are set up in towering bundles, like oversized sheaves, so they can reach up and tear the leaves off. It turned out that the boy's grandfather had told him in no uncertain terms, that morning at breakfast, that it is cruel to keep elephants in captivity, so he was going to see something dreadful.

"They should be back in the jungle, back in nature!" the child cried. "They have horrible lives! The people here hurt then! They beat them! I can't stand to think of them suffering!" He was crying so hard that he couldn't see the elephants as they peacefully demolished the tree branches.

Tim Delbosqu, the Knie elephant master, took pity on this child, and knelt to tell him the story of the baby elephant, Indi, over there, who had been taken into an elephant orphanage in India because her mother had been killed, and she would have died on her own; and about how the circus adopted her, so here she is in a herd of elephants again; her life is saved, and look what a good time she's having now. The child stared at Tim furiously. He didn't want to look at Indi. She seemed forbidden. "My grandfather," he sniffled, "wouldn't lie to me."

I felt immensely sorry for this child, who had been robbed of elephants; and so did Tim, who shook his head sadly, looking helpless. It seemed to me that the grandfather had corrupted his grandson — had ruined, that is, his capacity to read objects (the enclosure, the trees) clearly, much less the living creatures themselves. He could no longer attend to the dramatic and moving details, and the happy ending, of Indi's story, which happened to be true and about someone real, right before his eyes. The lies about suffering were more compelling. Inescapable, pervasive despair had been bestowed upon the child as a gift, and he was forced to treasure it. Human beings, we know, are very susceptible to the stimulations of pornography, and sometimes I think that this pornography of animal suffering is the worst, because its effect is to make it so hard to see straight or to think straight. I hate it especially when children are exposed to it, but grown-ups seem to do this deliberately, in good conscience, and to feel virtuous about it afterward.

The pornography of suffering is a cruel trick, based on ignorance, on estrangement of people from animals, a lack of familiarity and knowledge. And the people who campaign on this manipulative platform are remarkably ferocious in their refusal to face the consequences of their insistences, like the woman who longed to liberate the horses in the Bronx.

Several years ago, the Royal Society for the Prevention of Cruelty to Animals commissioned a renowned English animal behavior research scientist, Dr. Marthe Kiley-Worthington, to study the welfare of animals in circuses and zoos. The idea, ostensibly, was to bring some objective facts to bear in an area of intense and emotional controversy.

Accordingly, Dr. Kiley-Worthington spent eighteen months doing research, including more than three thousand hours of scientific observation and visits to fifteen circuses in England and one in Switzerland. She studied animals at rest, in training, traveling, and performing.

The result was an extensively documented, sensibly presented conclusion that on the whole circus animals lead good, happy, healthy lives, and that animals would be harmed, not helped, if their work in circuses were outlawed, or if the so-called animal rights lobby continues to put circus trainers out of business. She made practical suggestions for improving living conditions, while arguing against the damage to both animals and people caused by those who would abolish the tradition of animal performance. Such a campaign, she maintained, seeks to enforce a state of animal apartheid, in which people and animals would be kept rigidly segregated and separate from each other, to their mutual impoverishment and danger.

The RSPCA, upon receiving these conclusions, refused to publish them. One can only assume that these findings, no matter how rationally arrived at and substantiated, were incompatible with the RSPCA's agenda.

Dr. Kiley-Worthington subsequently paid to have her study published herself. *Animals in Circuses and Zoos: Chiron's World?* (Little Eco-Farms, 1990), a detailed and matter-of-fact little book about the daily lives of circus animals, holds steady above the furor which it aroused and which continues to surround these issues.

Anyone wishing to think seriously about all of these difficult matters should read *Adam's Task*, a splendid book in which Vicki Hearne addresses herself to, among other things, the right of animals to learn and to work, and our mutual rights of association. These are the true and crucial rights which circus celebrates.

Circus is diverse, sensual, rich. It is a live antidote to sterility and isolation. It welcomes the exotic, the bizarre. It brings us, safely encircled, into realms of wildness. The show before us does not display animals abstracted in scary words or charted numbers, or fixed in photographs; nor does it transform them into cartoon characters, stuffed toys, or accessories. It recognizes, instead, animals' stature, talent, expression, intelligence, and depth of relation. This show lets us know animals and lures us into more knowing, which is one definition of real love.

The consequence of *not* knowing is ominous: an empty world. If animals were no longer allowed to work in circus, I would argue, human beings might be disallowed, as well. I suppose there are people out there who would complain about the way Big Apple Circus women use and display their bodies; and the harangue would be made, no doubt, for the women's own good.

The tone which people use when they praise circuses for being without animals is heavy with exaltation in their own exquisite sense of higher virtue, when the only appropriate tone is one of mourning for what has been ruined and lost. Critics who say that animals don't belong in the circus have, I believe, a dour and pessimistic view of the world they're busy trying to perfect. They want things to be orderly, which is to say, disembodied. This seems to me to be a recoil from, and an affront to, the beauty and terror of creation itself. It reminds me that one of Hitler's first moves, in his passion for tidying up the messy world, was to round up all the gypsies. And I have no doubt that he was proud, then, of making the world a better place. You'd think we would know something useful, by now, about sterilized visions of the world, fueled by fear and piety, and executed by force of separation, exclusion, and control.

Animals in circus give us a way out of all this. Watching Toto and Peggy, Bill and Marie-Pierre and David, I thought, We *need* elephants. Or, watching the Liberty horses, *We need horses*. It's good to remember, through all the controversies, that people simply adore the animal acts. You don't see anyone leave to go to the bathroom or buy ice cream while animals are in the ring. There's a need for people to sit two feet from horses that come roaring past them and don't touch them; there's a need for people to have that kind of exposure to big animals. The refinements of tradition and training must endure as well. As we need the Spanish Riding School, or the American Ballet Theater, or other traditional centers of culture, circus animal work in its single ring must continue. It hasn't any other use than that we need it.

It's interesting, then, to think about all the ways in

which the contemporary taste for what is called "natural" can pressure aesthetic decisions with regard to animals, and at what cost. In circus, humans and animals perform as artists. We seldom give the animals credit for being professionals, with talents and skills and expressiveness. They make easy assumptions about what's natural wobble on their feet. Anna May, for example, wouldn't think one way or another about wearing a pink tutu, if this were part of her job, any more than Baryshnikov minds appearing in public in pink tights. In Anna May's case, a tutu does nothing to enhance her beauty, so it is a sensible aesthetic decision to have her go without. What if her athletic and dramatic talents were put to work in a pantomime which was a send-up of ballet dancers — would the tutu then be considered to be in poor taste? Probably, because at this moment many people don't seem to think it's funny when animals make fun of them.

Art exaggerates; the taste for naturalism exaggerates by its refusal to admit it's there at all. The effort to appear natural, to give an impression of being natural, may demand as much ingenuity in its execution, and be as problematical in its results, as all other aesthetic decisions. If the traditions of animal performance were to be altered to fit this taste, some complicated results would ensue. If it were important for the audience to think of animals as "natural," then the animals would appear uncostumed, unadorned, as close to naked as possible. If the notion of "dignity" were important, circus would show the animals dramatically lit and framed with dramatic music, but not doing very much at all, just standing about; they would have to appear to know nothing. The idea that "animals are happy to be here" would show them engaged in tail-wagging, romping, prancing, and other actions easily interpreted as joyful. If people wanted to know that "animals and people love each other" the animals and people would be shown hugging one another.

Ornamentation, to animals, is irrelevant, though a horse who loves to work certainly perks up when his tack appears. Milling about under lovely lights with little to do would not, to most animals, be a particularly interesting way to spend time. Animal happiness is often expressed in forms not easily read by people who are unfamiliar with them. (For example, just as you may not be able to recognize my joy if it doesn't take the form of smiles and laughter and you don't know me very well, you might not accurately read the ecstasy of a Border Collie working sheep, unless you know that his tail is low to the ground, then, and definitely *not wagging*.) Moreover, horses, and many dogs, do not like being hugged. I don't know what an embrace of her trunk or her leg would mean to an elephant. Big cats are not, strictly speaking, huggable at all.

Nonetheless, these animals could all be trained to *appear* to welcome these gestures, and to give all the requisite impressions. But by asking them to do so, we would require animals to become clowns. In a sense, that's fine, because clowns are good actors and hard workers; they reflect necessary truths, and some animals have always done good work as clowns. But it is not the only work for animals, and for some it is not their calling at all. Increasingly, however, and quite paradoxically, this is what circus is asked to do with all animals, regardless of their individual inclinations, by the pressure for the naturalistic.

I confess that I am myself quite hopelessly enamored of certain appearances. I prefer meadows, for example, with their diverse, disorganized grasses and unpredictable wildflowers, to formal seventeenth-century parterre gardens. But where I come from, hay meadows have to be fought for, with energy and skill, against the natural encroachment of second-growth forest, and through this struggle I've come to admire the impulses and ingenuity behind those geometric patterns of old, though I still don't want to construct them myself. Country life has sensitized me, perhaps, to matters of taste which necessarily carry so heavy a burden of the myths we need now.

I once had occasion to ask Slava Zolkin, the famous Russian bear trainer, whether it isn't unnatural for bears to juggle. He replied, "It isn't natural for *people* to juggle! Or to walk on the highwire! But people can do it because of their mental development. Because of their *education*. The same is true of bears. Look, I work with their *minds*; it's the *mental* development that's important in our work. Of course every bear has his own talents; some are better at some things than others. I live with them; it's my job to know them and discover each bear's character, his talent. I find out what each one has the ability to do well, and I build on that. That's what a good teacher *does*! One person might be good at riding a bicycle on a highwire and another"—he glared at me—"might be a writer! . . . Look, maybe I can say it this way: *Bears and people have it in their natures to use their minds*."

So I began to think about how it's people who are obsessed with the natural, because we are more easily persuaded (than, say, bears) to be pushed out of shape — to distrust thought.

What we really long for, and need, is *animals* — beautiful, various, whole, in the here and now — the exquisitely endless present in which they allow us to join them. Just as I might say myself — as I walk around and think about this, or sit and try to write about it — "I need an elephant! I need a horse!" as a way of longing for the Muse.

The shifting forms that flicker in the magic ring bespeak a chimerical Muse. Is she an elephant? (In which case I love to think of her in diaphanous draperies). Might she metamorphose into golden horses drumming our messages with their flying hooves? into an aerialist enacting the intricate details of a flying-dream far overhead in silver light? Or might she abide in a stooped and shabby bum, in a baggy suit and floppy hat, shuffling back and forth across the ring's edge? Whatever her form, one thing certain about the Muse is that you cannot command her to stay where you are. She's a wanderer.

The Thousand and One Nights has been full of changes: mysterious arrivals, disappearances. Now, in the finale, the whole troupe of wandering players bursts into the ring in a parade whose excitement is fueled by portents of departure. Their exuberant greeting says, We're hitting the road. The music is jazzy, a joyous din; bright light illuminates the ring, which fills with dancing people and animals, returning for their last bow as the ringmaster calls them by name. They strut the circle, saluting the crowd. Then they all gather at the edge of the ring, facing outward, grinning, waving, clapping and dancing in time to the music. It is an incitement. The audience joins in the rhythm of the clapping, swaying and stomping. The circle's circumference comes alive, as the performers push at the edge, stir up the concentric rings to mutual celebration, an exuberant give-and-take of revelry and farewell. It is a moving ritual of beauty on the move, and it feels like the most natural thing in the world to be part of it.

Taking a bow, in circus, means exchanging send-offs. The finale says that endings ought not to be inconspicuous, awkward, or constrained. Stiff bows and polite applause are no way for people to part, when they have brilliantly come together. If something wonderful has happened, don't let it go quietly! Don't pretend you haven't felt anything! I like to think of the raucous responses which Mozart's operas aroused, in a less puritanical age, and of the liveliness with which people might even now respond to classical music if they hadn't been trained to be so dismally well-behaved in concert halls. Brought up in the latter tradition, I was delighted when I first experienced the hoopla that attends the final bows in classical ballet—the flowers, cheers, whistles, as well as the flamboyant sweeping bows and curtseys of the dancers. The Big Apple Circus finale has some of the same atmosphere of courtly ritual, but this is a raucous, freewheeling court, full of jugglers, acrobats, fantastic beasts, and dancing out into the streets.

So many sizes, shapes, and colors, of so many nationalities, races, and species, have flashed past; their various virtuosities have played with extremes, leapt boundaries. Circus plays with time, drawing on ancient themes and elaborating them in visions that are wholly present and conscious. I remember the story of the medieval juggler who teased a smile onto the stone saint's face; ominous, ridiculous masked clowns leading the way into rites of death and renewal; Pan's passionate face, his seductive music, his dancing goat feet; the legend of animals speaking in human speech on Christmas Eve to honor the solstice's mystery of departing and renewing light. In my case, the circus makes me remember the animals I have known, their tangible mysteries, their lucidity; I mourn the animals I've lost (my lovely Keeper, a gray Arab like a circus horse, under the hill, now, and cantering circles above it), and I long for the ones to come. You will have your own memories, you own dreams.

Begin with the name, end with the name: circus, *le cirque*, the ring. A circle is a natural form, stressed and balanced, expressive of infinite motion and perfection, and having no end. To our great regret, the performers' jubilant snake dance winds its way out of our sight. Then Scheherazade darts back in, carrying her book, which she opens to an ornate page that reads: "The End." Then — she disappears.

But there's a joke here. Hasn't she said this before, a thousand and one times? Hasn't each of her endings had a hook in it? Night after night, the original Scheherazade banished boredom; she transformed impulses of control and death into those of affirmation and joy. This is why she and her stories are such perfect emblems of the art of the ring, where diverse animals and diverse people tread the same centered ground, where it's nonsensical, impos-

sible, to speak of circles ending, and where, against all op-
position, creatures may celebrate the world together. So
circus rises to the sacred poetic mission:

> *In the deserts of the heart*
> *Let the healing fountain start,*
> *In the prison of his days*
> *Teach the free man how to praise.*
>
> W. H. Auden
> "In Memory of W. B. Yeats"

Acknowledgments

The world of circus is essentially private. This is why I am particularly indebted to the people of The Big Apple Circus — to all of those, named and unnamed in this book, who for several years have granted me the pleasure of their company and conversation. If it were not for their tolerance and exquisite good manners, this book would not exist.

Other circus people have treated me with this same extraordinary patience and generosity of spirit: Mary Chipperfield and Roger Cawley, in England; Louis Knie, Fredy Knie, Jr., Chris Krenger, and Tim DelBosqu, at The Circus Knie in Switzerland; Slava Zolkin of The Moscow Circus; and David Balding and his colleagues at The Circus Flora in St. Louis, Missouri.

When I first saw Katja Schumann's training sessions, I knew this was the most splendid horse work I'd ever seen, in any discipline, anywhere. Her skill and gallant spirit make her the *sine qua non* of this book. Paul Binder has been my good teacher in all my thinking and learning about the art of circus. This most territorial of men (who once rumbled down at my dog, "This is *my* tent, Corgi!") has given me liberal access to important maps of his world, without which I would have been quite lost.

All of these people, in circuses here and abroad, have made me familiar with the distinctive atmosphere, combining extreme intensity and extreme calm, which they create, which an artist needs to thrive, and which I have come to love.

In the course of this work, I have had help from many people who have brought me joyously to regard the riding arena, the barn, the kennel, the dance floor, and the writing desk as locations on common philosophical ground. I bow to them all: Marie Borroff, Bianca Calabresi, John Craven, Deborah Dows, Marthe Kiley-Worthington, and Ernestine Stodelle. And of course there's Vicki Hearne, who is not only a brilliant juggler of words and ideas, but a good dog trainer, too; it's my good fortune that we are both so fond of working dogs and juggling together. I thank her for all these forms of conversation much as, in another kind of act entirely, a Labrador retriever might thank an Airedale with all her heart.

It was Monroe Price, in an act of errantry typical of him, who made it possible for this book to begin the leap from a private to a public existence. Very fortunately for me, Howard Boyer was the publisher who was there to catch it; the one who said, "Aha!"

I applaud Agie Sciarra, Mary Seaver, and Judith Straut for their staunch word-processing on my behalf. And Cathy Languerand has helped make this writing possible by her skilled work in house and barn — places which, like their respective inhabitants, she recognizes as inseparable.

Ivy Starr, the artist who made the pictures in this book, worked in wind, heat, dust, and rain. She sat in the hot sun for hours, contemplating elephants lounging confortably in the shade. She perched on a stool in the company of horses, using hay bales for a drawing table. She commuted to strange venues and kept peculiar and taxing hours. As she created her visual wonders, she once again gave me the example of her energy, skill, keen eye, and capacity for delight, for which I thank her, as ever.